TRUSTING
God's
Heart
WHEN YOU CAN'T TRACE
His Hand

TRUSTING
God's
Heart
WHEN YOU CAN'T TRACE
His Hand

John McLaughlin

CLC ❖ PUBLICATIONS
Fort Washington, Pennsylvania 19034

Published by CLC ❖ Publications

U.S.A.
P.O. Box 1449, Fort Washington, PA 19034

GREAT BRITAIN
51 The Dean, Alresford, Hants. SO24 9BJ

AUSTRALIA
P.O. Box 419M, Manunda, QLD 4879

NEW ZEALAND
10 MacArthur Street, Feilding

ISBN 0-87508-592-X

This printing 2002

Printed in the United States of America

Contents

Chapter   **Page**

Preface 7

1. Jesus Loves Me, This I Know 9

2. God Tested Abraham 25

3. "Take Your Son, Your Only Son,
   Isaac, Whom You Love" 39

4. On the Third Day . . . Abraham Saw the Place 49

5. "Stay Here While I and the Boy Go Over There" 63

6. "Father, Where Is the Lamb?" 75

7. Abraham Bound His Son
   and Laid Him on the Altar 85

8. Abraham . . . Took the Knife to Slay His Son 93

9. "Now I Know That You Fear God" 103

10. Moriah . . . The Manifestation of God 115

11. "I Will Surely Bless You . . .
    Because You Have Obeyed Me" 121

12. He Was Called God's Friend 133

Dedicated to Jessie . . .

A God-fearing mother who truly valued
the importance of bringing up her children
in the House of the Lord . . .

From her eternally grateful son

Preface

*T*HE crucifixion of Jesus Christ lies at the heart of God's message to a suffering and hurting world. Through the story of the Cross, God openly and passionately displays His love for the fallen sons of Adam. And though we find in the Holy Scriptures that God is sovereign, Calvary assures us that every decision our sovereign Creator makes, He makes out of an infinite and unchanging love for those He created in His image.

Though life is fraught with many troubling questions which we don't yet have answers for, the truth that *"God so loved the world that He gave His only begotten Son"* serves as an anchor for those who find themselves questioning their Creator's love while being battered by life's storms. I'm confident that the story of the Cross will put to rest any nagging doubts about our Creator's love if we'll but embrace its liberating truth.

Because Christ was *"the Lamb slain from the foundation of the world,"* it's only natural that we should find its message foreshadowed in the pages of the Old Testament Scriptures. Indeed, it is found there in many forms. But perhaps the most vivid and moving example of its foretelling is found in the twenty-second chapter of the book of Genesis. The heart-rending story contained in this historic passage—the call for Abraham to sacrifice his son Isaac—speaks of not just an earthly father and his son, it goes beyond these finite, human characters to unfold an eternal love story involving our heavenly Father and His only Son. In this stirring chapter God masterfully paints a picture of His love on the canvas of human emotion so we might better understand the magnitude of that love which compelled Him to make the supreme sacrifice.

It's my earnest desire that through this writing you may look beyond the characters of Abraham and Isaac to view the story of the Cross and, in so doing, come away with a new appreciation of God's immeasurable love for man. I trust that at the conclusion of this book, you too will be able to say: "*God is too kind to ever be cruel and too wise to ever make a mistake. Though I might not always be able to trace His hand, I can always trust His heart.*"

1

Jesus Loves Me, This I Know

"*In this meaningless life of mine I have seen both of these: a righteous man perishing in his righteousness, and a wicked man living long in his wickedness. . . . There is something else meaningless that occurs on earth: righteous men who get what the wicked deserve, and wicked men who get what the righteous deserve*" (Ecclesiastes 7:15, 8:14). King Solomon was deeply troubled by life's inequities. It made no sense to him that righteous men suffer while godless men prosper. Although it's been nearly 3,000 years since Solomon penned these words, it's a question that many of God's children still have difficulty reconciling with their faith. After all, if our all-powerful God is also a God of perfect justice, why would He allow such inequities?

Because of life's many injustices, it is imperative that Christians everywhere come to implicitly trust their Master's heart. Indeed, without the utmost confidence in our Creator's love, life's inexplicable inequities can quickly give rise to doubt, doubt to discouragement, and discouragement to defeat. *There is no greater enemy of our faith than unanswered questions about God's love.*

Our adversary, the devil, knows this full well. He began his temptation of man by dropping a seed of doubt into Eve's mind regarding the loving intentions of her Creator. When Satan suggested that God was withholding something good from her when He had commanded that she not eat of the forbidden fruit, he was not only challenging her Creator's right of authority but also the sincerity of His love. And because Satan was able to successfully plant this insidious doubt in Eve's mind while she was yet in the midst of Paradise, how much easier is it for him to seduce this fallen and weakened race now that we're surrounded by the ills of Paradise lost! Satan's primary tactic in his warfare on mankind is still centered upon the question of God's love. He knows that if we are uncertain of our Creator's love, the very foundations of our faith are fatally flawed and will never stand firm through life's storms.

I believe the world-renowned theologian Karl Barth clearly understood this principle. It's told that when once asked by a group of reporters what he felt was the greatest discovery he had ever made, he quickly replied, "*Jesus loves me, this I know.*" Since they were anticipating a profound and complex answer from one who had spent a lifetime contemplating lofty ideas, they could hardly believe what they had heard. After overcoming their initial shock to such a simple reply, one brave reporter asked the learned Doctor, "You mean, sir, that the greatest theological truth you've ever discovered is 'Jesus loves me'?" "No," Barth replied, "not 'Jesus loves me'. . . 'Jesus loves me, *this I know.*'"

In his follow-up question the reporter had completely overlooked what was most crucial to this long-time theologian. He had stated only in part what Dr. Barth considered to be his greatest and most precious discovery. Over the course of many years he had come to learn that "Jesus loves me" must first *be embraced by our hearts before its power is released in our lives.*

Even though God does love us, without the personal connection, without this absolute *assurance*, the mere *fact* of that love will neither calm our troubled souls nor heal our broken hearts. It is only as we personally come to know and trust God's love that we can then draw our strength from the bounty of its grace. Indeed, the faith of many has been shipwrecked on the rocks of distrust and despair simply because it had not been securely anchored to God's love.

Hardships, injustices and persecutions can quickly shake the faith of those who are uncertain of their Creator's love. But for the one who can say without reservation, "Jesus loves me, *this I know,*" that person shall find strength and comfort enough for any storm he might ever face. He needn't worry that the winds of adversity will cause his faith to be battered against the rocks of unbelief, for his unshakable confidence in the Creator's love will keep his ship safely on course. In the most tempestuous seas, his faith will be guided by the calm assurance that God has His children's best interests at heart even though the storms rage on.

According to the very teachings of Scripture, there will surely be times when we will find ourselves battered about by seemingly unending storms that have arisen from no fault of our own. In fact, they may have suddenly come upon us while we were actually doing what God had commanded. We must not think this strange, for it was at the command of Christ Himself that His obedient disciples once found themselves in the midst of a life-threatening storm. This happened soon after He had told them to get into a boat and row across the Sea of Galilee. But it was in the midst of that journey—*in the act of obedience*—that a fierce storm arose. It wasn't because they'd disregarded Christ's directives and consequently placed themselves in danger. They had, in fact, launched their boat at the Master's command. Nevertheless, even though they had been obedient, they found that their obedience had landed them in the center of a violent storm.

It's also important to note that when Jesus—who had remained behind to pray—was alerted to their struggle, He didn't immediately calm the wind and waves. Rather, He chose to allow the storm to continue in all it's fury while He walked out to them on the raging sea. And at first His terrified disciples thought that what their eyes saw was only an apparition. Jesus had to call out, "Take courage! It is I. Don't be afraid." Peter then said, "Lord if it's You, tell me to come to You on the water" (Matthew 14:28). So if we would rightly learn the lesson contained in this real-life incident, we must not overlook the fact that Jesus did not quiet the storm *before* Peter stepped out. Instead, He had him come while it was yet in full force!

But why hadn't Christ calmed the sea before bidding Peter come? Hadn't he and the other disciples battled the storm long enough? Because John later tells us of Peter's swimming prowess (John 21:7–8), it is easy for us to now understand Christ's actions. If Jesus had not allowed the storm to continue, Peter's getting out of the boat would have required no faith; it would have demanded no risk. If things hadn't worked out once he'd gotten out and away from the boat, all Peter would have had to do was simply swim back to safety.

The fact that Jesus did allow the storm to continue forced Peter to look to something other than himself for his safety and success. Peter had to trust the *voice and heart* of Him who called from the midst of the storm. As a seasoned fisherman, Peter knew his strength was no match for nature's fury.

Thus, if Peter was to move out in faith while the storm

continued, he would have to possess an unshakable confidence in the One who commanded him to come—a confidence based not only on Christ's ability, but also on His *dependability*. It's one thing to be certain of one's ability to back up what he's said, yet quite another to know that he'll come through when your life is on the line. Each of Christ's followers must have this complete assurance of His love if they too would hope to walk on the water while the storms rage on.

Now as it was with Peter, so shall it be with all Christ's followers. At times He allows His children to face insurmountable odds which require a strength and wisdom they simply do not possess. But He permits this so they might learn to rely upon His all-surpassing strength and wisdom and not upon the frailty of their own resources.

At this point it's profitable for us to recall the words of the Apostle Paul when he wrote: "The foolishness of God is wiser than man's wisdom, and the weakness of God is stronger than man's strength" (1 Corinthians 1:25). That's why Paul could go on to write in his second letter to the church at Corinth: "I delight in weaknesses, in insults, in hardships, in persecutions, in difficulties, for *when I am weak*, then I am strong" (2 Corinthians 12:10). Paul had come to understand that it was only when he had come to the end of his own limited resources that he would truly become strong. For it was then that he would be forced to depend upon the only One who possessed unlimited resources.

Earlier in this second letter, Paul had recounted for them one such time when his own meager resources had been completely exhausted: "We do not want you to be uninformed, brothers, about the hardships we suffered in the province of Asia. We were under great pressure, far beyond our ability to endure, so that we despaired even of life. Indeed, in our hearts we felt the sentence of death. *But this happened that we might not rely on ourselves but on God, who raises the dead.* He has delivered us from such a deadly peril, and He will deliver us" (2 Corinthians 1:8–10).

When Paul said that these life-threatening pressures happened so he might not depend upon himself but upon God, we can assume that he too knew the story of Peter and the storm. And since Jesus had allowed Peter to come to a place where he would be forced to rely wholly upon the Lord, it would be logical for Paul to conclude that for this very same reason Christ might allow others to go through similar difficulties.

The many hardships Paul encountered in his early missionary endeavors drove him to an ever greater reliance upon God. He found he must depend upon the Lord if he was to bear up under the tremendous pressures of each new day—if he was to "walk on water" while his storms raged on. Paul was well aware that he had been given the treasures of the gospel *within a "jar of clay"*—a vessel that could easily be broken. But he had also learned the secret of success: "I can do all things through Christ who strengthens me" (Philippians 4:13 NKJV). Because he believed and practiced this truth, he was then able to write: "Though we are hard pressed on every side, *we are not crushed* . . ." (2 Corinthians 4:8).

A simple illustration from science might better help us understand what Paul meant by "not being crushed." Physics teaches us that water is highly incompressible and therefore will lend incredible strength to what otherwise is quite weak. For example, if we should fill a glass bottle (one free of all defects) with ordinary tap water, corking it off at the top while allowing no air to remain trapped within, we could then use this fragile container to drive nails. Why? Because of the strength of the *glass*? Certainly not! The secret lies in the bottle's contents. Even though we strike the nail with great force, the bottle will not shatter because the incompressible water within won't allow the glass to collapse in upon itself. Instead, the nail is driven into the wood!

Thus, because of what *fills* it, the bottle can be used for what would otherwise destroy it. Likewise, as the Christian allows his life to be filled with the Spirit of Christ, he—through this Living Water—can also do what would otherwise crush his jar of clay. "Greater is He that is in us than he that is in the world!" (1 John 4:4).

Notice also that in the midst of his difficulties Paul does not beckon his own defeat by telling himself a discouraging story. What someone once wisely noted, Paul had already learned: *We do not live with just the facts of our lives. We also live with the story that we tell ourselves about the facts of our lives.* In truth, the story we tell ourselves is even more important than the things which have actually happened to us.

From this insightful observation we can deduce that the most influential person who speaks with us day in and day out is none other than ourself. For no one else has either the time or the opportunities to converse with us at such length or in such depth. Therefore, what we tell ourselves during those times of fear, hurt, stress or loss will most certainly determine whether we experience victory or defeat, joy or sorrow—whether we become a *victim* or a *victor*.

In this instance Paul said, "This happened that we might not rely on ourselves but on God, who raises the dead." He didn't say that this happened because everyone and everything was against him, or that God had forgotten or forsaken him. Paul never called into question God's love. Quite the contrary was the case. He reasoned that this incredible pressure came his way so that he might exchange his weakness for God's strength and his folly for God's wisdom. If we looked at our difficulties through the same eyes of faith, we would soon discover the secret to Paul's ability of consistently rising above the inequities and hardships of life.

When Paul wrote these things, he was not covering up his problems, pretending all was well. The life-threatening pressures that surrounded him would not allow him to deny their reality. He acknowledged the fact that he was in circumstances far beyond his ability to endure. But when finding himself there, he affirmed to himself the things that would strengthen his spirit, not break it.

In contrast though, many of us when placed in the midst of difficult circumstances often recount to ourselves those things that weaken our faith and diminish our hope. We become like Jacob of old, who, even though at one time he had wrestled with the Angel of the Lord, later allowed himself to forget that he was the chosen one of God Almighty. The storms of life had worn away at his faith.

You might recall that it all begins for Jacob when his favorite son Joseph is sold into slavery by his jealous brothers. They then bring back to their father the special robe he had given him. But before presenting it to Jacob, they rip it and stain it with the blood of a goat. With feigned sorrow they bring it before their father, asking if this is indeed Joseph's coat—giving the false impression that his favorite offspring had perished in a savage attack by some wild animal. Their plan succeeds and Jacob goes into deep and prolonged mourning.

Some years later a devastating famine envelops the land where Jacob and his family live. Now although a famine might catch God's people off guard, we may be assured it will never surprise Jehovah Jirah—which, translated, means: *The Lord Our Provider.* As Corrie ten Boom has said, *"There's never panic in heaven . . . only plans."* In His infinite wisdom and love, God had already made divine provision for Jacob and his family by using a most unlikely means: the jealousy of Joseph's brothers which led them to sell their own flesh and blood into slavery.

When Joseph does arrive as a slave in Egypt, once again God chooses a most improbable tool and a most unlikely method to move him into a position where he might be noticed by Pharaoh. God has a man named Potiphar buy him as a slave so his immoral wife—thwarted and infuriated by Joseph's impeccable morals—might have him imprisoned on trumped-up charges of attempted rape.

Again, what might appear to man as a downward step is in fact quite the opposite. For it was through a series of events that occurred while Joseph was in prison that Pharaoh hears of his great wisdom. After Joseph correctly interprets Pharaoh's troubling dream, he is immediately made Egypt's Secretary of Agriculture!

Jacob had no idea that God had sent Joseph ahead to spare them all from certain starvation. All he knew was that Joseph was no longer by his side and that the land God had promised him could now not even feed his own family. Added to this painful situation was the problem of how to get more grain from Egypt. When his sons had gone there earlier, the man in charge of Egypt's grain distribution (Joseph in disguise) had taken hold of one of the brothers (Simeon) as an accused spy. He then had proceded to tell them that he would not give them any more grain unless they proved their story by bringing back their youngest brother, Benjamin.

This last demand brought everything to a head, for Benjamin was not *just another brother*, but he had now taken Joseph's place as his father's favorite. So unbeknownst to Jacob, God was forcing him to face his greatest fear . . . *the loss of another son.* Jacob was afraid that what had happened

to Joseph might one day happen to Benjamin. This past loss
daily cast its ominous shadow over the present, robbing Jacob's
house of its rightful blessings. Jacob was held hostage by the
trauma of the past while paralyzed by the fear of the future—
but God wanted Jacob free!

When Jacob first heard the ultimatum "Release Benjamin or face starvation," we find him audibly voicing what
he had already been telling himself in his heart: "Joseph is
no more and Simeon is no more, and now you want to take
Benjamin. *Everything is against me!*" (Genesis 42:36). Jacob
had lost all hope. He had allowed his circumstances to conquer his spirit. Through the pain of loss he had forgotten
that his God was *El-Shaddai . . . God Almighty.*

What a stark contrast between these words of Jacob and
those of Paul. Not only did Paul say "This happened that we
might not rely on ourselves but on God who raises the dead,"
but he also boldly proclaimed in Romans 8:28, "We know
that in all things God works for the good of those who love
Him, who have been called according to His purpose." Unlike Jacob, rather than looking at *what* was against him, Paul
looked at *Who* was for him. Therefore, he could confidently
declare in verse thirty-one of this same chapter, "If God is
for us, who can be against us?"

As this chapter in Jacob's life comes to a close, we find
him learning that Joseph is not only alive and well, but also
the keeper of Egypt's grain! We must not, however, pass over
this small yet most important scriptural observation: "The
spirit of their father Jacob revived. And *Israel* said . . ." (Genesis 45:27–28).

Even though years earlier God had given Jacob the name
Israel, meaning "You have struggled with God and with men
and have overcome," Jacob later found *himself* overcome. He
had wrestled with discouragement and had lost. The spirit of

Israel, which had prevailed in its struggle with God and with man, had now been conquered by the storms of life. But it had not been conquered by what had actually happened but by the story he had told himself about what had happened: "Everything is *against* me!" The *spirit* of Israel had been defeated by the *stories* of Jacob. Not until he saw the proof that Joseph was alive and well did the conquered spirit of Israel rise from the pit of despair.

So Jacob did not simply live with the facts of his life, he also lived with the story he told himself about the facts of his life. Indeed, it was the story he told himself that became even more important than the facts themselves. It was what he told himself that kept him a slave to the pain of the past and the fear of the future. And unlike Paul, who declared "Nothing can separate us from the love of God," Jacob had come to the conclusion that life's storms had indeed separated him from the blessings and promises of his God.

Now let's return to Peter's situation. Soon after he had gotten out of and away from the boat, his faith began to waver. Matthew records that when Peter saw the wind he was afraid and began to sink. Immediately he cries to Jesus, who quickly reaches out a saving hand. The instant Jesus brings him safely back into the boat, the storm ceases.

Herein lies the lesson: That night Jesus proved Himself Master *in* the storm and Master *of* the storm. *In* the storm, for He walked on the sea; and *of* the storm, for He calmed its fury. Let us then take comfort in this fact: When things are out of *our* control, Jesus has it all in *His* control. It's also important to note that the first thing Jesus said to His disciples that night had absolutely nothing to do with calming the *outward* storm, but everything to do with calming the *inward* storm. "Take courage!" He said; "It is I. Don't be afraid" (Matthew 14:27). In saying this, He directs the dis-

ciples attention away from the *terror* of the storm so they
might find peace through the *Master* of the storm.

These stories were written down for our instruction and
encouragement. Therefore, we can be assured from this incident that no matter how difficult our way becomes, we should
not be dismayed. Although the Prince of Peace may not
always choose to calm our storms, He will always come to us
in the midst of them. At *His* bidding, we too can walk on
the raging sea. That night this truth was indelibly imprinted
upon the heart of each disciple . . . a lesson that would
forever hold the key to their future success. Jesus knew they
must never forget that no matter how dark the night or
terrible the storm, He would not let them perish. For this
reason He did not teach the lesson by mere words, but rather
by the adversity of a life-threatening storm. Through His
actions that night He assured them that He loved them too
much to ever leave them on their own.

Without the personal assurance of God's love we can
never hope to build that trusting relationship with Him which
will take us safely *and* triumphantly through life's storms.
The simple fact is that without trust, we will not triumph.
Where trust is lacking, fear will conquer faith and we'll find
ourselves inadvertently playing into our enemy's hands. Panic
will grip our hearts and we'll end up running *from* our source
of help rather than *to* our source of help. Instead of waiting
for the Lord's provision, instead of looking for His deliverance, we'll attempt to find our own route of escape. Driven
by fear, we'll perish in the storm.

It is this same trust, rooted in the assurance of God's
love, which must also undergird our faith if we're ever to be
consistent in our obedience. This is especially true if our past
obedience—like that of the disciples—has taken us into the
eye of the storm. Without trust, instead of obeying those

commands which we fear might possibly *sink our boat*, we'll find ourselves constantly questioning God, afraid He does not have our best interests at heart.

Whenever God's love is called into question, trust will be lacking . . . and wherever trust is lacking, obedience will eventually be compromised. We can never be consistent in our obedience when we have lingering doubts about our Savior's love. Sooner or later a lack of trust will produce a breakdown in obedience. And where there is a breakdown in obedience, all hope for spiritual gain is lost. As F. B. Meyer once said: "Each step of real advance in the divine life will involve an altar upon which some dear fragment of the self-life has been offered."

In other words, in order for Christian growth to occur we must be brought to the altar of sacrificial obedience. We cannot expect to grow in the knowledge and character of Christ until we're ready to obey His directives *regardless of the cost*. But without trust, we will be extremely hesitant to pay such a price. *If we are to advance in His divine life, then we must be convinced of His divine love.*

The trust, then, that is necessary for both our success and growth rests upon the assurance of God's love. That's why *Jesus loves me, this I know* is the greatest theological truth anyone can ever discover. With the revelation of this truth comes the *freedom* to trust God in the midst of any storm and the *will* to obey Him even when obedience requires great personal sacrifice. Those who are confident of God's love know that any storm they might ever face, they face in the shadow of His loving presence; and however difficult the path of obedience becomes, it will always lead to their advancement in the divine life.

Indeed, when we are certain of God's love, storms are no longer a source of fear, nor obedience a troublesome thing.

His love has taken the risk out of our obedience and the terror from our storms. In commenting upon the importance of this personal assurance of our Creator's love, Charles Spurgeon once remarked, "God is too kind to ever be cruel and too wise to ever make a mistake. Though we might not always be able to trace His hand, we can always *trust His heart.*"

To the church at Rome we find Paul writing these words that were absolutely essential for his own faith and for the faith of all who would be victorious in Christ:

> Who shall separate us from the love of Christ? Shall trouble or hardship or persecution or famine or naked-ness or danger or sword? As it is written: "For Your sake we face death all day long; we are considered as sheep to be slaughtered." No, in all these things we are more than conquerors through Him who loved us. For I am convinced that neither death nor life, neither angels nor demons, neither the present nor the future, nor any powers, neither height nor depth, nor anything else in all creation, will be able to separate us from the love of God that is in Christ Jesus our Lord (8:35–39).

Notice Paul does not say, "*escaping* all these things we are more than conquerors"—as most would prefer it read—but rather, "*in* all these things we are more than conquerors *through Him who loved us.*"

In the following pages, we will learn more of the width and length and height and depth of God's love as prophetically depicted in Genesis 22. For the deeply moving story contained in this historic passage—the call for Abraham to sacrifice his son Isaac—speaks of not just an earthly father and his only son, but goes beyond these finite, human characters to unfold an eternal love story involving our heavenly Father and His only Son, Jesus.

In this stirring chapter God masterfully paints a picture

of His love on the canvas of human emotion so we might better understand the magnitude of that love which compelled Him to make the supreme sacrifice . . . a sacrifice He made 2,000 years after the one recorded in Genesis. Christ Himself spoke of this when He declared, "For God so loved the world that He gave His only begotten Son that whosoever believes in Him should not perish but have everlasting life" (John 3:16 KJV).

In making this declaration of God's love, Christ included all and excluded none. Take heart! God's intentions are clear: He longs for all to arrive at the place where they may confidently proclaim that the greatest, the most liberating and the most reassuring truth they've ever come to discover is "Jesus loves me, this I know."

$$2$$

God Tested Abraham

 ome time later God tested Abraham. He said to
him, "Abraham!" "Here I am," he replied. Then God
said, "Take your son, your only son, Isaac, whom you
love, and go to the region of Moriah. Sacrifice him there
as a burnt offering on one of the mountains I will tell
you about."

Early the next morning Abraham got up and saddled
his donkey. He took with him two of his servants and
his son Isaac. When he had cut enough wood for the
burnt offering, he set out for the place God had told
him about. On the third day Abraham looked up and
saw the place in the distance. He said to his servants,
"Stay here with the donkey while I and the boy go over
there. We will worship and then we will come back to
you."

Abraham took the wood for the burnt offering and
placed it on his son Isaac, and he himself carried the fire
and the knife. As the two of them went on together,
Isaac spoke up and said to his father Abraham, "Father?" "Yes, my son?" Abraham replied. "The fire and
wood are here," Isaac said, "but where is the lamb for
the burnt offering?" Abraham answered, "God Himself

will provide the lamb for the burnt offering, my son." And the two of them went on together.

When they reached the place God had told him about, Abraham built an altar there and arranged the wood on it. He bound his son Isaac and laid him on the altar, on top of the wood. Then he reached out his hand and took the knife to slay his son. But the angel of the Lord called out to him from heaven, "Abraham! Abraham!" "Here I am," he replied. "Do not lay a hand on the boy," he said. "Do not do anything to him. Now I know that you fear God, because you have not withheld from Me your son, your only son."

Abraham looked up and there in a thicket he saw a ram caught by its horns. He went over and took the ram and sacrificed it as a burnt offering instead of his son. So Abraham called that place The Lord Will Provide. And to this day it is said, "On the mountain of the Lord it will be provided."

The angel of the Lord called to Abraham from heaven a second time and said, "I swear by Myself, declares the Lord, that because you have done this and have not withheld your son, your only son, I will surely bless you and make your descendants as numerous as the stars in the sky and as the sand on the seashore. Your descendants will take possession of the cities of their enemies, and through your offspring all nations on earth will be blessed, because you have obeyed Me" (Genesis 22:1-18).

If you were living in the United States during America's cold war with the Soviet Union, you will certainly remember these familiar words that were frequently interspersed throughout the radio broadcasts of that era: "In cooperation with the FCC, for the next thirty seconds this station will conduct a test of the Emergency Broadcast System. This is only a test." What followed was a long, annoying, uninterrupted tone, after which the announcer would conclude by saying that in the event of an actual emergency you would have been told where to tune your radio.

Because this was a time when we were living with the constant fear of an imminent nuclear attack by the Soviets, did you ever think what your reaction might have been if you hadn't heard those all important words: "This is only a test." Fear? Panic? Confusion? I don't know about you, but those five words—*this is only a test*—meant the world to me (or better yet, that it wasn't the "end of the world" for me). The fact that I did know it was only a test kept me from being overcome by fear, panic or confusion.

How unlike Abraham's testing. He had no idea as to what was happening! God hadn't said to him, "Don't worry, Abraham, *this is only a test*. It's not the real thing. I won't require you to actually plunge the knife into your son's heart. All I'm asking is that you do everything up to that point."

How amazing it is to see that Abraham did not need to know the outcome before obeying the command. He promptly set out with his son on a mission of death in spite of his almost certain feelings of fear, confusion and panic . . . feelings that could not easily be ignored . . . feelings that appealed to both his logic and his love.

Do we respond as Abraham did when God calls us to the mountain of sacrifice? Or do we demand to know beforehand whether or not we must truly bring down the knife upon that which is most precious to us? Do we want to know if God is actually going to require a sacrifice of us before we begin our climb up the mountain? Often we wish to learn *prior* to our mission what the outcome will be, lest too late we discover that in our obedience we've lost the very thing we never really intended to surrender at all. Obviously though, for God's testings in our lives to be valid we must not be privy to such foreknowledge.

In Proverbs 17:3 God reveals an all-important principle regarding His testings: "The crucible for silver and the furnace for gold, but the Lord tests the heart." Here Scripture teaches that just as the crucible and furnace are not meant to destroy these precious metals but rather to refine them, so the testing of the Lord is never meant to injure His children but rather to purify them.

Peter, in explaining why trials are a necessary part of the believer's life, writes, "These have come so that your faith— of greater worth than gold, which perishes even though refined by fire—may be proved genuine and may result in praise, glory and honor when Jesus Christ is revealed" (1 Peter 1:7). In commenting on this verse Kenneth S. Wuest in *Word Studies in the New Testament* lends this added insight:

> The picture here is of an ancient goldsmith who puts his crude gold ore in a crucible, subjects it to intense heat, and thus liquefies the mass. The impurities rise to the surface and are skimmed off. When the metal worker is able to see the reflection of his face clearly mirrored in the surface of the liquid, he takes it off the fire, for he knows its contents are pure gold. So it is with God and His child.*

Scripture makes it clear that God has one goal in mind for all His children . . . that we "be conformed to the likeness of His Son" so He might see His own divine nature clearly reflected in our lives. And how better could this be accomplished than by God taking His children through the fires of testing so the blemishes in their characters might be exposed and the impurities in their faith be extracted?

Another passage of Scripture dealing with God's testing of man is found in Deuteronomy. There Moses declares to Israel, "Remember how the Lord your God led you all the

---

* Wuest, Kenneth S. *Word Studies in the New Testament*, Grand Rapids, Mich.: Wm. B. Eerdmans Publishing Company, 1973, page 27.

way in the desert these forty years, to humble you and to test you in order to know what was in your heart, whether or not you would keep His commands. He humbled you, causing you to hunger" (Deuteronomy 8:2–3). Here God tells us that He will allow us to undergo difficult, stressful times to test the commitment of our hearts. He desires to know if we are truly obedient or simply "conveniently" obedient—if we're equally committed to His will whether the times are good or bad, pleasurable or painful.

I'm afraid, though, that when things are not going as well as we would like, we often display the same type of obedience to our heavenly Father that disgruntled children have learned to give to *their* parents. Perhaps you've heard the story of one such boy and his "obedience":

"Billy" was a five-year-old who possessed the unbounding energy that boys his age seem to have, yet never find enough hours in the day to deplete. As a result they're constantly storing up this excess energy— meaning that, to every mother's dismay, their "Billy" is constantly accumulating an ever greater reserve of unspent energy, just to add to the next day's already inexhaustible supply.

Unfortunately, during one Christmas season Mom made a grave error: she took this bundle of unspent energy with her for some last-minute shopping. Because of the lateness of the hour, the pressures of the season and her already frayed nerves, she was in no mood for Billy to be anything but obedient. While hurriedly looking through the housewares department, she ordered Billy to stay right by her side at all times. Now this sounded like a reasonable request, at least under normal circumstances, but these circumstances were anything but normal. After all, Christmas was but a few days away. Besides, the housewares department just happened to be located next to the toys.

Needless to say, the temptation was just too great for Billy. He left her side not once, not twice, but three times to survey the "promised land." After his third reconnaissance Mom was about to explode! Taking Billy by the nape of the neck she hurried him over to the nearest bench and there firmly deposited him with this final threat: "Billy," she said sweetly between clenched teeth, "if you so much as even move your bottom from its present position, you may never again have a bottom to move . . . Do you understand!!?"

Well, Mom had pulled out the "heavy artillery." Billy knew his weapons were no match for hers for he had only a slingshot, she a bazooka. Even "little David" would not have gone up against such odds. So there he sat. Yet before she was out of earshot, he bravely slung one last stone: "I may be sitting down on the outside," he said, "but on the inside, I'm still standing up!"

Do we at times see our own "obedience" mirrored in Billy's? Do we display outward acquiescence while our hearts remain unsurrendered? If so, then we've failed to understand the true meaning of obedience. When it comes to matters of God's kingdom, the heart is all important. During His time among us, Jesus emphasized the necessity of a surrendered heart when He said, "These people honor Me with their lips, but their hearts are far from Me" (Mark 7:6). He also taught that out of the heart flow the very issues of life. "The good man," He said, "brings good things out of the good stored up in his heart, and the evil man brings evil things out of the evil stored up in his heart" (Luke 6:45).

As a loving Father, God's primary responsibility is to ensure that we possess pure hearts wholly surrendered to Him. Only then can we manifest His divine character that's being developed within us. And only then might the world see our good deeds and "give glory to our Father in heaven" (Matthew 5:16). Whether it's Abraham, Israel or ourselves, God will test the heart to determine the depth of commitment. While that test is proceeding, He will do all within His power to purge it from every impurity.

The subject of testing inevitably brings us to Job. As his story opens we find Satan standing before God's throne calling into question the sincerity of Job's piousness. He tells God that the only reason Job faithfully serves Him is because He's handed him life on a "silver platter." Consequently, God allows the devil to test Job's faith by permitting him to bring mass destruction upon him and his entire family. If this were not enough, God leaves His faithful servant in the dark. Job hasn't the slightest clue as to why he's experiencing such tremendous sorrow and suffering.

Day and night he cries out to the God whom he has faithfully served . . . yet the heavens are silent. When God finally does answer Job, He makes no mention of that which was happening behind the scenes—that He's allowing Satan to put Job's righteousness to the test. God simply declares to Job His eternal power and wisdom and, therefore, His sovereign right to do whatever He pleases.

It's also worth noting that God did not dispute Satan's challenge when he claimed Job's uprightness to be only the superficial product of a sheltered and blessed life. The Lord Himself knew that for obedience to be authenticated it required some measure of personal cost, for it's easy to obey when there's no price to pay.

Even of Jesus, Scripture records, "Although He was a son, He learned obedience from what He suffered" (Hebrews 5:8). Therefore, let us not be led into the false assumption that our obedience will escape such testing. Though the depth to which Job's faith was tested is the exception and not the rule, nonetheless, the principle of proving our obedience through personal loss or hardship is still in force.

Eventually God gives Job the understanding as to why his life was battered about by such calamities. But before Job was enlightened, the only answer to his questioning was a deafening silence from heaven. He wasn't able to read of his own glorious ending, how "the Lord blessed the latter part of Job's life more than the first" (Job 42:12). How difficult it must have been for him to continue on in faith when he knew no reason for his pain.

As we look at the testings of Abraham and Job, the lesson is clear: Neither the understanding to our testings, nor the blessings that are there for those who are victorious, ever come *before* the fact. Until we've completed the test, we're required to walk in hope—hope that confidently awaits an unseen reward. And of this hope Paul writes, "Now to see is no longer to hope: why should a man endure and wait for what he already sees? But if we hope for something we do not yet see, then, in waiting for it, we show our endurance" (Romans 8:24–25 NEB).

Our testings, then, shall be times in which we cannot see, times in which we do not have an answer to the question *"Why?"* "Why, God, is this happening to me? Why, God, are You standing afar off? Why, God, would You require such a sacrifice of me?" During testings, we are called to walk in darkness. Obviously this will exert tremendous pressure on our faith, tempting us to take matters into our own hands, urging us to seek our own route of escape, to provide our own source of light. But Scripture warns of giving in to such pressure: "Trust in the Lord with all your heart and do not rely on you own understanding" (Proverbs 3:5).

Through the prophet Isaiah we find this word of encouragement, immediately followed by one of warning to those who find themselves faced with the darkness of uncertainty:

"Who among you fears the Lord and obeys the word of His servant? *Let him who walks in the dark, who has no light, trust in the name of the Lord and rely on his God.* But now, all you who light fires and provide yourselves with flaming torches, go, walk in the light of your fires and of the torches you have set ablaze. This is what you shall receive from My hand: You will lie down in torment" (Isaiah 50:10–11).

To trust in the name of the Lord is to trust in His nature, to rely upon His loving-kindness even though we can't make any sense of what might be happening. To repeat the words of Spurgeon: "Though we might not always be able to trace His hand, *we can always trust His heart.*" We must not forget this axiom: *Understanding is God's responsibility, trusting is ours.*

As it was with Abraham and Job, so shall it be with us. We must continue to walk in the way of obedience and righteousness even when that path is obscured by the fear of loss or the terror of the unknown. In spite of what our natural inclinations might call for or our human reasoning demands, we must not give in to these impulses. We must not succumb to their unrelenting pressure nor yield to their deception. We must not allow fear to override our trust and pull us off the path of obedience. At all cost we must continue to hold fast our confidence in our Creator's love. We must refuse to play into the enemy's hands by abandoning our trust in the truth of God's Word and the faithfulness of His nature. Even if reason and reality should shout to the contrary, we must turn a deaf ear to their cry.

As previously noted, God would use these difficulties in the lives of His people for the refining of their characters. His desire is that *through* all these things we become conformed to the image of His Son. It is only when our faith is tested that Christlike character may be formed within. James said, "Consider it pure joy, my brothers, whenever you face trials of many kinds, because you know that the testing of your faith develops perseverance. Perseverance must finish its work so that you may be mature and complete, not lacking anything" (James 1:2–4).

Note that it's not simply our faith which brings about the desired results—it's the *testing* of our faith. An untested faith is incapable of producing Christian maturity. That's why James could say, "Consider it pure joy when you face trials of many kinds." It's not that the Christian is joyous because he's under fire; rather, he rejoices in the assurance that the result of his faithfulness under fire will ultimately bring about in his life that which he and his heavenly Father desire.

When as Christians we go through these difficult times, we often use this passage from James to encourage ourselves and others. Frequently, however, its lesson is heard but not heeded. We've become so familiar with its words that we unintentionally ignore its admonition. Here James is specifically addressing the Christian's *attitude* when faced with trying times. He admonishes us to cultivate an attitude of joy in the midst of our struggles.

Early in my Christian journey God taught me to apply the truth of this verse. The lesson began the day our family decided we needed a bigger car. Each time we went somewhere we felt as though we were the proverbial sardines packed into a can—our "can" being an extremely small subcompact which our family of four had squeezed into for the last five years.

One day we received a phone call from my wife's mother who was visiting family in Oklahoma. She told us that one of her relatives was selling just the car we were looking for— a large station wagon in excellent condition. Although it was several years old, it had low mileage. And they were selling it at a price we could afford. Receiving their assurance that it was as good as it sounded, we bought the car and my mother-in-law drove it back to Los Angeles. After "our gift from heaven" arrived, it took a mere two weeks for us to painfully discover that the phone call we thought had originated in heaven might have actually originated from a place *much* further south. The car that we were told had low mileage in fact had just the opposite. After hearing ominous sounds emanating from beneath the hood, we researched the engine's serial number. To my dismay, I discovered someone had replaced the original engine with one that was nearly ten years older than the car itself!

I was seething, for I knew I was going to "lose my shirt" over this car. Then to add insult to injury, I was informed that the relatives who had sold us the car had owned it for only a short time and were truly ignorant of the scam. I felt utterly helpless, realizing there was no recourse for our situation. Because my mother-in-law felt it to be all her fault, she offered to buy back the car. But we knew that this would have placed an undeserved financial burden on her. So after using all our resources to purchase this "junkyard reject," there we were, still squeezed into "the can."

As I sat in my office angrily assessing the situation, I heard that "still small voice" speak to my soul: "Count it all joy when you meet with various trials." "Lord," I quickly retorted, "You don't need to remind *me* of that verse. I know it quite well!" Once again the voice came gently to my heart, but this time bringing with it a different verse: "Do not merely listen to the Word . . . Do what it says" (James 1:22).

Even though James was the author of both those verses, I had never before linked them together until that moment. In the past, when I considered what it meant to be a doer of the Word, it was always in terms of some tangible act like feeding the hungry or visiting the sick, never in terms of my attitude. Now for the first time I realized that in my present circumstance, obedience on my part demanded *I possess a joyful attitude in spite of what had happened.*

As I determined to be a doer of the Word and not just a hearer, I began to thank God. But not to thank Him for what had happened, but rather for the fact that regardless of how bleak the situation appeared, He had not abdicated the throne. Because the King of all the universe was also my heavenly Father, I knew I could trust Him to work this out for my good and His glory if only I would do my part and *"count it all joy."*

As you might imagine, my commitment to maintain this joyful attitude and be an obedient doer of the Word was tested quite often. But when tempted to complain, I would quickly remind myself that I must continue to do that which lay within *my* power—to "count it all joy"—and then be patient to let God do what was in *His* power—to work this for my good and His glory.

After what seemed to be a very long time but in fact was only a matter of weeks, I received the following note in the mail from a couple who had once attended our church, but whom I had not seen or heard from in quite some time. The gist of it was this: *"Dear Pastor John, Recently we came into some extra money and felt impressed by God to share it with you. . . . In Christ, Bill and Cindy."* A check was enclosed.

When I received that note, I was sitting at my desk as I was a few weeks earlier. At that time I was grumbling at my ill-fortune. Now I was rejoicing! As I sat there and wept, I couldn't help but reflect upon the Lord's faithfulness in re-sponse to my simple obedience to His gentle promptings. The amount of the check not only made up for the loss on the car and enabled me to purchase another, but it also covered the entire amount of a recent pledge to missions my wife and I had made!

So the source of joy in the midst of our trials comes not from our present circumstances but from our future hope. Lest we begin to form an errant theology, however, we must understand that it's not merely a hope that God will ultimately get us what we want; it's a far greater and more substantial hope. It's a hope which knows that if we'll persevere when tested, this will develop within us Christlike character. Nothing in the world can come close to matching this blessing! Therefore, we rejoice in the midst of difficulties, not because of what is happening *to* us but because of what is happening *in* us.

Thus, testing is an essential element in every Christian's life for it is *the* path to Christlikeness; therefore, it's also the reason for our rejoicing. When God declares that He withholds no good thing from those who walk uprightly (Psalm 84:11), let's not forget that *good* may be defined in terms of what is produced in time rather than what's happening at the present, and what's taking place within rather than what's happening without. Unfortunately, though, in our age of instant gratification I'm afraid the Church has mistakenly believed in a form of "microwave Christianity" that in a minute's time can bring us into Christlikeness. Words like *perseverance* and *endurance* are now just ancient relics from the vocabulary of yesterday's Church.

3

"Take Your Son, Your Only Son, Isaac, Whom You Love"

God promised Abraham and his wife Sarah a son. But long after her child-bearing years had passed, Sarah was still without a child and Abraham without an heir. Then, when all seemed hopeless, three angelic visitors came and announced that Sarah would give birth within a year. Abraham's and Sarah's first response was to laugh at such a thought. After all, the idea did seem so preposterous . . . so impossible. And so, upon his birth, they named this "miracle child" Isaac—meaning *"laughter."* This name would serve as a continual reminder that they had laughed at the promise of God.

Though at first this name was given because of their unbelief, later the name Isaac took on added meaning for this elderly couple. Isaac truly became their source of joy and laughter. His presence brought a fresh breath of life to this previously barren home. So when God called Abraham to surrender Isaac, He was not simply asking him to sacrifice something *from* his life, but rather to sacrifice the very thing that meant more to him than life itself. God was asking Abraham to offer up that which was dearest to him—the joy and laughter of his heart!

The Lord was testing Abraham to see if anything stood between him and his devotion to God. He knew if Abraham would give up Isaac, then there was nothing he would not surrender in his service to God. Yet, in the final analysis, Abraham was only asked to give back to God that which he had first received from God. Even as King David said when he and his people had given so generously for the future construction of the Temple: "Everything comes from You, and we have given You only what comes from Your hand" (1 Chronicles 29:14).

During His sojourn among us, on at least one occasion Christ reminded us that God is still asking for the surrender of that which is nearest and dearest to our hearts. In the synoptic Gospels we find a rich young ruler falling on his knees before Christ and asking what he must do to inherit eternal life. Jesus responds by telling him to obey the commandments. "Which ones?" he asks. After Jesus lists several commands the young man replies, "All these I have kept. What do I still lack?" Jesus answers, "If you want to be perfect, go, sell your possessions and give to the poor, and you will have treasure in heaven. Then come, follow Me" (Matthew 19:20–21).

In His directive Jesus was bringing this wealthy young man face to face with the core issue of his faith. In stating the commands He did, Jesus purposely left out the greatest of all . . . the command upon which all others rest. If we fail to obey this command, whatever other Christian duties we might well perform, our noncompliance to this one command will disqualify us in our quest to please God. That command being: "You shall love the Lord your God with all your heart, soul and mind" (Matthew 22:38).

The young man had failed to keep this one supreme

command. He had allowed his wealth to become the first love of his life. Jesus knew that within this young ruler's heart the love of God had been supplanted by the love of money. In telling him to give up his riches Jesus brought him face to face with this reality of his divided loyalty and, thus, his failure to obey the greatest of all commands.

In Mark's account it says, "Jesus looked at him and *loved* him" (10:21). Here, the Holy Spirit is making it clear that it was not some sadistic, cruel side to Christ's nature which commanded that the inquirer give up his wealth. On the contrary, it was His great love that compelled Him to make such a strong demand. Jesus knew that the young man's riches had become a snare to his soul and a poison to his spirit. He knew his love of money would forever keep him from the divine fellowship Christ had come to bring.

Furthermore, the young ruler's earthly wealth would be his to keep for only another fifty or sixty years at best. But what Jesus would grant in return for his obedience—giving his earthly treasure to the poor—would be "treasure in heaven," his for all eternity. Listen to how William Barclay in *The Daily Study Bible Series* describes the connection that exists between earthly and heavenly riches:

> Upon earth you are in charge of things which are not really yours. You cannot take them with you when you die. They are only lent to you. You are only a steward over them. They cannot, in the nature of things, be permanently yours. On the other hand, in heaven you will get what is really and eternally yours. And what you get in heaven depends on how you use the things of earth. What you will be given as your very own will depend on how you use the things of which you are only steward.*

* Barclay, William, *The Daily Study Bible Series*, Philadelphia: Westminster Press, 1975, page 209 (Luke's Gospel) (First published by The Saint Andrew Press, Edinburgh, Scotland, 1956).

This is what Jesus meant when He said: "Do not store up for yourselves treasures on earth, where moth and rust destroy, and where thieves break in and steal. But store up for yourselves treasures in heaven, where moth and rust do not destroy, and where thieves do not break in and steal" (Matthew 6:19–20). And again He declared, "Sell your possessions and give to the poor. Provide purses for yourselves that will not wear out, a treasure in heaven that will not be exhausted, where no thief comes near and no moth destroys. For where your treasure is, there will your heart be also" (Luke 12:33–34).

Notice also that after Jesus gave the rich young ruler the command to give away all his riches, He said, "Then [after you've been obedient] come, follow Me." Dietrich Bonhoeffer rightly noted in *The Cost of Discipleship* that often we presume we may follow Christ while continuing to hold fast to what He's commanded we surrender. But we only deceive ourselves when we imagine we can follow and yet not obey. To love the Lord our God with all our heart, mind and soul requires we relinquish all that we *are* and all that we *have* to His divine directives. Any less of a commitment only shows we do not truly understand this greatest of all commands.

Lastly, we must note that when this young man turned to walk away, even though the heart of Christ must have been breaking, He did not soften His demand. He did not say, "Would you consider giving half your riches away? If not, then what would you deem acceptable?" God is not open for negotiations when it comes to obeying any of His commands, let alone the greatest of all commands. Just as Abraham and this ruler were asked to surrender what was most precious to them, so down through the centuries God has required each of His followers to lay at His feet everything that would exalt itself above the love of God.

But there's another "Isaac" involved in this story—the heavenly Isaac—the only begotten Son whom the Father had delighted in before the beginning of time. The earthly Isaac was a type of the heavenly Isaac, for through Abraham's obedience God would illustrate how He Himself would offer up for us the *joy* and *laughter* of His heart. Long before His Father led Christ up Calvary's hill, He would have His servant Abraham take his only son up the mountain of sacrifice to prophetically enact the story of the Cross. And as Abraham was commanded to give not just one of his many servants but his *only son*, the *unique one*, so our heavenly Father did not simply offer up one of the millions of celestial beings who stand ready to serve at His beck and call. But when He gave His sacrifice, just like Abraham He surrendered His only Son. When the Father sent Jesus into this fallen world, He gave heaven's richest treasure and left the vaults of Paradise empty. He brought to a world of sorrow and pain the everlasting *Joy of Heaven*—the eternal laughter of His heart.

During my childhood my parents required that I share my possessions with others. Often I would do so with great reluctance, and only after selecting a toy which meant little or nothing to me. Then I would pass it off to my unsuspecting playmates, hoping that this "magnanimous" gesture on my part would both satisfy my parent's request and keep my friends preoccupied so as not to discover that I'd actually kept the good stuff for myself.

As adults we often transfer this childlike attitude into our Christian service. We, like Israel of old, would offer God the "leftovers" of our lives (Malachi 1:6–14). We too would foolishly attempt to bring Him the blind and lame as our "sacrificial animals," hoping He will be distracted by these second-rate gifts so we might keep for ourselves the things we truly hold precious. But unlike man, God cannot be fooled.

Just as He saw through Israel's pretense, so He now sees through ours. And just as these gifts were unacceptable to Him then, they are still unacceptable today.

It's also important to keep in mind that God is not asking us to do what He Himself was not willing to do. He unhesitatingly surrendered what was dearest to Him. And the amazing thing about God's gift is the fact that "while we were still sinners, Christ died for us" (Romans 5:8). As John wrote, "This is love: not that we loved God, but that He loved us and sent His Son as an atoning sacrifice for our sins" (1 John 4:10). Unlike God who gave this glorious gift even to His enemies, we, as we bring our treasure to Him, are placing it at the feet of the One who loves us best—One who is more than deserving of whatever sacrifices we make.

Some of us have experienced those times when we've known that our families and friends wouldn't fully appreciate the sacrifice that lay behind the giving of our gift, but that did not keep us from making the sacrifice. It was our love which compelled us to give. So it was with God. He knew that we could never fully comprehend the personal cost involved. But despite our inability to appreciate His gift, in love He surrendered His most prized possession—His only Son.

On the other hand, when we offer to God the things dearest to our hearts, He knows their worth and will forever value the sacrifice we've made. This is clearly shown in the vow God made with Abraham immediately after he had surrendered his most precious gift: *"I swear by Myself, declares the Lord, that because you have done this and have not withheld your son, your only son, I will surely bless you and make your descendants as numerous as the stars in the sky and as the sand on the seashore. Your descendants will take possession of the cities of their enemies, and through your offspring all nations on earth will be blessed, because you have obeyed Me"* (Genesis 22:16–18).

It's often been said that we can never outgive the Lord. Indeed it would be absurd for us to imagine that we could ever match God's gifts to us, let alone think that we could surpass them. And just as we can never come close to outgiving the Lord, neither can we ever come close to *"outloving"* the Lord. Because His love for us is immeasurably greater than our love for Him, the gifts He lavishes upon us from the storehouse of His unlimited treasures are far greater than any sacrifice we might ever render to Him.

It was not long ago that I became quite concerned about our financial future. My wife and I owned no home and had no savings. And as far as a retirement account, we had less than $10,000 in a voluntary fund that was set up for the ministers of our denomination. To add to this somewhat gloomy outlook, there was the possibility that Social Security would not be there when we "baby boomers" retired. So during my prayer time one morning, I was running this scenario by my heavenly Father. But rather than receiving from Him the sympathy and support I felt I desperately needed, I sensed Him telling me that I was to focus on giving and not on getting.

Well, this was not at all what I had wanted to hear and neither did I think it would be what my wife wanted to hear—especially if I was to be the messenger! I felt like we needed some sympathy and support—not a challenge to give more! I had forgotten that God's ways are not our ways; He then proceeded to remind me of His teaching on this subject from the Sermon on the Mount:

> "Do not worry about your life, what you will eat or drink; or about your body, what you will wear. Is not life more important than food, and the body more important than clothes? Look at the birds of the air; they do not sow or reap or store away in barns, and yet your heavenly Father feeds them. Are you not much more

valuable than they? . . . The pagans run after all these things, and your heavenly Father knows that you need them. But seek first His kingdom and His righteousness, and all these things will be given to you as well. Therefore do not worry about tomorrow . . ." (Matthew 6:25–26, 32–34).

And so on that very morning I sincerely told my heavenly Father that I wanted to be a better giver.

Soon after I had this talk with God, my wife and I were at a banquet where we were challenged by the evening's speaker to do more for the worldwide advancement of God's kingdom. He encouraged all of us to give more generously of our finances so that more and more Christian literature might be printed and distributed for the propagation of the gospel message. That night as we were lying in bed talking about the events of that evening, I told my wife that I believed God had spoken to me about us becoming better givers. After some discussion, together we told the Lord that during the next 12 months we would like to double our giving to world missions. On the practical side of this, it would mean that we would need to give several thousand dollars more than our personal budget could bear. So we asked the Lord to supernaturally provide these funds by giving us this extra money through whatever means He might choose.

Not only did we receive in the pursuing 12 months more income through monetary gifts than we'd ever received before, but by year's end we had been given an additional $2,000 above and beyond what we'd committed to give! But that's still not the end of the story. In December of that year a former member of our congregation came into the church office, a man now actively involved in the ministry of one of our sister congregations. He asked if I had a moment to talk.

We went into my study, where he told me about a trust fund he had set up to feed the needy women and children of

Africa. It was set up to last twenty years and currently had many millions of dollars in it. He believed me to be an honest man, he said, and would like me to serve as an extra set of eyes to look over the monthly financial statements. Then he asked if I might be willing to take an occasional trip to Africa so I could see firsthand how the funds were being dispersed. He mentioned that he was getting older and wanted to make certain that this work would continue on if God should call him home. Humbled, I told him I'd be glad to help in any way I could. He then told me that I'd be receiving a substantial monthly income for my part in this charitable endeavor. I replied that this was not necessary. His response was simply, "It's already a done deal!" So for the next 19 years it appears that my wife and I will be getting a healthy addition to our monthly income. Through this personal experience it has become even more clear to me that we can never outgive God, for we can never *outlove* God!

4

On the Third Day . . .
Abraham Saw the Place

*A*t first light, on the very day after he received the Lord's command, Abraham began the most difficult journey of his life. What a remarkable thing it was that without any delay or hesitation he should began a mission that was to culminate in his own son's death! This, however, was not the first time Abraham had faithfully set out at God's command. Forty years prior to this journey the Lord had said to him, "Leave your country, your people and your father's household and go to the land I will show you" (Genesis 12:1).

In this command the Lord instructs Abraham to leave the comfort and security of his homeland and set out for an *unknown* destination given by an *unseen* God. Nevertheless, at the word of the Lord, Abraham obediently moved out. But even though he was setting out on an uncertain journey, he was not going into an *unplanned* future. In the final analysis, Abraham's journey was simply one man's faith moving him safely along an already charted path—a path that had been predetermined by an omniscient God: one who declares, "I am God, and there is no other; I am God, and there is none like Me. I make known the end from the beginning, from ancient times, what is still to come" (Isaiah 46:9–10).

I want to take a moment to share with you a personal story that powerfully illustrated to both my son and me how the faithfulness and protection of our omniscient God does indeed go before His own. It began one Sunday evening after he and I had hitched up a trailer to his Chevy Blazer and began what we thought would be an uneventful two-hour trip. We were going to pick up at my mother's house a piano that she had recently given to my son. Well, about 45 minutes into the trip the trailer came loose from the ball and began thrashing back and forth behind us, with only the safety chain keeping it from totally breaking away. At the time this happened we were in the center lane of Interstate 5 in heavy traffic, traveling at about 60 mph! My immediate concern was that the trailer might break the safety chain and that we could not get it to the shoulder of the freeway without endangering the other drivers. But it seemed that just as quickly as these thoughts came, the chain broke!

It was then I began to cry out, "Jesus help us, Jesus help us!" I felt for certain there would be a major pileup behind us, resulting in serious injuries and even possible fatalities. As I was calling out to God, I was also frantically searching for my cell phone so that we could contact the California Highway Patrol. It seemed like forever, but in what was probably less than five minutes I had reached the CHP dispatcher, who informed me that they had already received a call about the trailer. It had taken us about a quarter mile to get over to the shoulder of the interstate. We jumped out of the Blazer and began walking back to where the trailer had come to a stop. To our surprise, all five lanes of the freeway were shut down and the CHP was already on the scene!

When I approached the nearest officer, I learned that

someone close behind us had seen what was happening and immediately began working his vehicle from lane to lane until he had stopped all northbound lanes of traffic. The officer told us to bring our vehicle back to where the trailer was so we could hitch it back up and pull it off the freeway. But when we got there, we found that it had been damaged too badly for that.

Just then my heart sank—as I noticed that only a few yards behind the trailer there was a car whose front end had been nearly pushed back to its windshield. Feeling the worst had happened, I anxiously asked the officer if anyone had been hurt. He told me that the car's air bags had deployed when it struck the trailer and the lone driver was fine! Instantly my anxiety was replaced with joy!

While waiting for the tow truck to come for the trailer and the CHP to complete its investigation, my son and I went back to our vehicle to collect our thoughts and give thanks to our God.

After a few minutes, my son looked back and noticed the officers putting handcuffs on the driver of the wrecked car. Needless to say, this seemed quite odd. We felt that if anyone were to be "cuffed," it should have been us! So I walked back to the nearest officer and asked why the man was being arrested. He told me that he had been "driving while under the influence of alcohol." I quickly processed this information and came to the conclusion that if anyone should have run into our trailer, he was the ideal man! For who knows whether or not he would have injured someone else later that night? Or possibly, as the result of this accident, the courts would now keep him from endangering the safety of others by revoking his license or placing him on probation.

But there is yet more to this remarkable display of God's

wonderful providence. As we were finishing up the paper-
work with one of the officers, I noticed there was another
pickup truck near the shoulder that was missing one of its
front wheels. I assumed that the driver of this vehicle also
must have hit something while trying to avoid the trailer or
the drunk driver. But when I asked the officer if this driver
had hit either the trailer or the other driver, he replied, "No,
she was slowing down for the traffic break and her wheel
came off!" Again I quickly processed this information and
came to the conclusion that had it not been for this accident, she might have lost her wheel soon afterwards—but
not while slowing down for a traffic break but while traveling at 60 to 70 mph!

As my son and I continued on our way that night—
minus one trailer—we had gained a new and profound appreciation of our loving heavenly Father's divine protection
and guidance. Even though we had single-handedly been the
cause of shutting down the entire northbound lanes of Interstate 5 coming out of Los Angeles, we knew that this traffic
nightmare brought to both of us a real-life example of how
our Creator goes with us, before us and behind us when we
put our trust in Him!

Two final footnotes: Afterwards my son told me that if
the trailer had not broken loose when it did, he would have
been unable to keep control of his vehicle. For he was not
only doing all within his power just to keep it in his lane,
but he felt that the thrashing of the trailer was going to spin
the vehicle totally out of control! Thank God that He can
break both the natural and spiritual chains that would otherwise destroy our lives! When we called home to tell my wife
what had happened, she asked us at what time this accident
took place. When we informed her of the time, she told us
that she and a friend had an unusual burden to pray for our

safety at that very hour! Thank God for the prompting of His Holy Spirit and their obedience to pray.

The psalmist bears witness to this personal assurance of divine providence when he writes: "You discern my going out and my lying down; You are familiar with all my ways. . . . If I rise on the wings of the dawn, if I settle on the far side of the sea, even there Your hand will guide me, Your right hand will hold me fast. . . . All the days ordained for me were written in Your book before one of them came to be" (Psalm 139:3, 9, 16). So Abraham's journey of faith had been carefully and lovingly planned long before it ever began. And because his going out was by divine *providence*, it would surely end in divine *blessing*.

But remember, Abraham's call to blessing was inseparably linked to the exercising of his faith, a faith which demanded he believe that the future blessings of obedience were far greater than the accumulated wealth of the present. To obtain the promised blessings Abraham had to obey the Lord's command to "go out" and leave behind his homeland, his people, his family, his friends—in short, everything which contributed to his sense of security.

The command to "go out" still remains the *only* avenue for obtaining God's richest blessings. All our goals and desires—indeed, the very course of our lives—must be placed at the Master's feet. Jesus said, "Any of you who does not give up everything he has cannot be My disciple" (Luke 14:33). But lest we think this to be an unusually harsh demand, we must realize that it is in fact the *love and wisdom* of God which calls us to "go out." He knows that as long as we're quietly at rest amid favorable, undisturbed surroundings, our faith lies dormant. But when we're pushed out from our secure setting, when we must leave our comfort zone, then we're forced to trust wholly in the Lord and the seed of our faith can begin to grow.

As it grows, the things which are unseen increasingly become more real to us than the things which are seen, for such is the nature of faith. This, of course, is exactly what God has intended, for Scripture says, "No *eye* has seen, no *ear* has heard, no *mind* has conceived what God has prepared for those who love Him . . . but God *has revealed it to us by His Spirit*" (1 Corinthians 2:9–10).

Faith is the medium through which the Spirit communicates. Thus, God will be persistent in His efforts to stimulate our faith so we might better hear the voice of His Spirit. He knows that faith is *the* key to understanding and experiencing all of His blessings. Only faith can apprehend the things of eternity. Paul tells us that "we live by faith, not by sight. . . . So we fix our eyes not on what is seen, but on what is unseen. For what is seen is temporary, but what is unseen is eternal" (2 Corinthians 5:7, 4:18).

Furthermore, the command to "go out" also forces us to cast away our "crutches"—those things which keep us hobbling through life. As long as we're "leaning on the arm of flesh," as long as we're depending on people, position or possessions for our strength or security, we will never experience true freedom. We'll forever be bound to that which keeps us from *running* the race of faith.

As indispensable as our "crutches" may seem, they will impede our progress, for no matter how proficient one becomes with crutches, they still remain just crutches. Only through Abraham's departure did he begin to discover that there would be no limit to what he could achieve, for he had left his "crutches" behind and had transferred his trust from that which only partially compensated for his weakness to the One who knew no weakness. The more we rely upon God, the stronger and freer we become.

God taught me this foundational lesson in faith soon after I had taken a position as youth pastor at a small rural church. Before this I was employed by a major airline and my wife was working in a dental office. We had just purchased our own home and were doing rather well financially. So when my wife and I made the decision to enter youth ministry on a full-time basis, we were careful to count the cost as best we could. We knew that besides adjusting to a totally different lifestyle, it would also require that we move out of an area in which we had both gone to school, leaving our home church and friends behind, and taking a major cut in pay. But after much prayer and discussion we felt we had "the mind of the Lord," and so we took the plunge.

Shortly after we'd made the move, however, there appeared a "small fly in the ointment." Unbeknownst to us, the church that had hired us was barely meeting its bills. Needless to say, when I learned of this, it caused me a great deal of concern—especially when I thought of my wife no longer working, our two-year-old son, and a baby on the way.

Soon after hearing this distressing news, I remember playing out in my mind what might happen if the church wasn't able to meet its bills. The scenario ended up being quite brief and rather frightening—I would be laid off! Then I really began to worry! What would I do? Where would I go? How would I pay *my* bills?

It was then that God's "still small voice" interrupted my anxious thoughts and brought with it the perfect peace that only He can give. My heavenly Father answered my fears in the form of a simple and direct question: "Who's responsible for your paycheck?" Instantly I understood: *He* had called, therefore *He* would provide. God would not be so cruel as to take us from our "homeland" only to leave us on our own. From that moment on I never again worried about the church meeting its payroll.

The story, however, doesn't end there. Before my wife and I had taken this position as youth pastors we had made a monthly commitment to world missions. Now, even though our income had decreased dramatically, we felt it would be a step of faith and an honorable thing to continue to give the same amount. This decision sounded so noble and seemed so spiritual—that is, before the Sunday that reality set in.

I was sitting on the platform and the pastor had just stepped to the pulpit to remind everyone that this was Mission Sunday . . . the Sunday we were to give our monthly gift. Though I was sitting there, dutifully playing the part of a model youth pastor and looking every bit the "cheerful giver," I was anything but *cheerful* on the inside.

As I sat there muttering to myself about not having the money to give, I was suddenly convicted about my attitude. I threw up a quick prayer to the Lord that went something like this: "*God, forgive me for my murmuring and complaining. I thank You for the privilege of helping to send Your gospel around the world.*"

Well, nothing had changed except my attitude. But that's all I had control over. I had to trust God to work out the rest. This He did immediately! As I exited the sanctuary that morning, one of the members shook my hand and said, "Happy Birthday!" As he did this, he filled my hand with money!

Now no one had announced that morning that I recently had a birthday, so I'm still not certain how this man knew. But his timing was perfect, or should I say *His* timing was perfect! When I got to the car, I looked to see how much I'd been given. As I quickly counted it out I found it to be the very amount of our monthly mission commitment!

But that's still not the end of the story nor the end of

the lesson. You see, there was a certain man in the congregation who from time to time would give us money. It wasn't something that happened regularly, but it did happen enough for us to know that he was concerned about our family's finances. Maybe it stemmed from the fact that he was a member of the church board and knew what we were being paid. Whatever the case, he was sensitive to our financial situation.

One day I was visiting this man in his home and he asked how we were doing. Well, I "milked" it for all it was worth, hoping his wallet would be opened as well as his heart. A couple of days after my visit with him I received some cash in the mail along with an unsigned note of encouragement. But God would not let me get away with it.

I knew I had "used" my brother and offended my heavenly Father, so the next day I returned to "the scene of the crime," but this time to "eat some humble pie." After I had fully confessed my trickery, the brother quietly said, "I'm pleased to see such honesty, but I wasn't the one who sent that money." Talk about feeling foolish! But it was well worth it, for it was a lesson well learned. God saw I was going back to my "crutches," depending once again on someone other than Him. He was much too loving to let me do that—to let me go back to my own personal Ur, that place from which God had called Abraham and was now calling me.

Even though Abraham's first journey demanded a giant step of faith, it paled in comparison to God's next requirement. Although his first journey meant leaving his old life behind, this one demanded much more. Now he was being asked to kill the precious, promised seed of the new life he had found. Yet if Abraham had not taken that first journey of faith, he would never have been prepared for the present one. His first journey helped nurture in him the much greater faith now needed for the successful completion of this one. Before Abraham could trust God with his only son, he would first have to trust Him with his own future.

This is God's way of developing ever greater faith within His children. If we should fail to trust Him in our first journey, it is unlikely that we shall ever have the courage to advance into deeper levels of obedience. The degree of obedience which Abraham obtained placed him foremost among the heroes of faith.

Today in our lives, like yesterday in Abraham's, God would call us to ever-increasing faith and thus to ever-increasing honor and blessing. Therefore our journeys of faith do not become less arduous with time. On the contrary, their successful completion will require ever-greater faith and ever-deeper trust. But the good news is that with each successful step we take into ever-increasing faith, there shall await us ever-increasing blessings.

The Bible says, "On the *third* day Abraham looked up and saw the place in the distance" (Genesis 22:4). In other words, Abraham was given time to carefully consider what God had directed him to do. God did not want His servant to simply act on impulse or emotion, so He gave him the space of three days to thoroughly think through the most important decision of his entire life. During this journey, Abraham had ample opportunity to reconsider what he was about to do. God wanted to know if Abraham would be steadfast in faith and unrelenting in obedience—if indeed he would finish what he had begun and finish it with unwavering resolve.

Those three days were the most difficult Abraham would ever have to endure. Imagine if you can the emotional trauma this father underwent as he lay by the campfire each night watching his young son sleep peacefully by his side, totally unaware of his father's true mission. Isaac did not yet know that his father wasn't taking him to the place of sacrifice to simply *participate* in the offering of a lamb, but he was taking him there to *be* the lamb. How could this father continue on this journey and how could he possibly explain its fatal ending to his only son?

As God dealt with Abraham then, so He continues to deal with His children today. He wants us to follow His directives as the result of a deliberate act of our faith, not as the result of an emotional moment in life. God would not have us make commitments to Him based only upon some momentary impulse, for He knows that too often those commitments which come from a temporary excitement fade with time.

How many times have we made these types of promises to God, only to discover too late that they were not made from an unwavering faith but an inconsistent feeling? Afterwards we found ourselves regretting our decision and eventually going back on our word. This kind of double-mindedness only brings condemnation to us and dishonor to God. He would rather have us be certain that what we purpose to do, we neither falter in nor turn back from until we have fulfilled our mission.

Jesus said, "No one who puts his hand to the plow and looks back is fit for service in the kingdom of God" (Luke 9:62). And again, "Suppose one of you wants to build a tower. Will he not first sit down and estimate the cost to see if he has enough money to complete it? For if he lays the foundation and is not able to finish it, everyone who sees it will ridicule him, saying, 'This fellow began to build and was not able to finish'" (Luke 14:28). We must keep in mind, though, that this unswerving resolve is not fashioned in a moment's time, but rather is forged in the furnace of deliberation.

Just as Abraham's decision was made only after careful deliberation, so it was with our heavenly Father. His decision to offer up His Son, to make Him the sacrificial Lamb who was slain for mankind's redemption, did not come as an afterthought to His plans nor as the result of an emotional impulse in time. His decision to surrender Jesus came as a carefully calculated forethought *before time began.*

In First Peter we find Christ described as "a lamb without blemish or defect . . . chosen *before the foundation of the world*" (1:20). And John calls Jesus, "the Lamb that was slain from the creation of the world" (Revelation 13:8). Thus the Apostle Paul declares, "God chose us in Christ before the creation of the world to be holy and blameless in His sight. In love He predestined us to be adopted as His sons through Jesus Christ" (Ephesians 1:4–5). God's commitment to man was a deliberate decision He made "before the foundation of the world"!

Since God made provision for our redemption before fashioning the world, then God's creative acts must have been the result of His desire to give, not to get—to please, not to possess. In his first epistle, John defines this fact of God's nature by just three simple words . . . "God is love."

At the heart of love lies the longing to give. Because "God is love," He wanted to give of Himself. Thus He made all that *is* so He might lavish upon His creation the beauty, goodness and glory of His own divine nature. We see this clearly displayed in all His wondrous works. God did not create out of a sense of loneliness or boredom, as some might think. He created out of His longing to *give.* Because the driving force behind His creative acts was love, as He worked His way up through the order of life He began pouring more and more of Himself into His works until finally, at the end of the sixth day, He declared, "Let Us make man in Our image." Thus, in the creation of man, God's love was finally and fully satisfied of its need to give.

But that pure and infinite love which compelled our Creator to give so deeply of Himself also drove Him into taking the greatest risk of all. From the moment God breathed the breath of life into man, man became the offspring of God in the truest and highest sense of the word. Because of this relationship, coupled with man's God-given ability to think, reason and choose for himself, it now lay within man's power to either bless or break the heart of God. Because God's love found its fullest expression in the creation of man, this creature could now bring to his Creator immense pain and grief—and all too soon we did. "It repented the Lord that He had made man on the earth, and it grieved Him at His heart" (Genesis 6:6 KJV).

When we look at the original language of this verse, we find that it paints a powerful picture for the reader. The word that is translated *repented* has as a part of its meaning "to sigh or breathe strongly," and the word that is translated *grieved* has as a part of its meaning "to carve at with a knife." So we might then paraphrase this verse as follows: "The sin of man caused a great knife to be plunged into the heart of God—and He gasped for air." The wounding of His heart was the price our loving Creator was willing to pay when He chose to make us in His image. Therefore we must always remember that each time we violate God's commands it is more than just the breaking of a law, it's the wounding of a heart . . . the heart of the One who loved us before the creation of the world.

5

"Stay Here While I and the Boy Go Over There"

With his beloved Isaac by his side Abraham started up the mountain where, in a few short moments, he would painfully and privately complete his obedience. It would have been far more bearable if God had simply required him to surrender his own life rather than that of his son's. Every loving parent knows it's much more difficult to watch your child suffer than it is for you to suffer. But for this father it was even more unbearable; for not only would he be unable to suffer for his son, he himself would be the *cause* of that suffering. Abraham would now grasp the instrument of his own son's death in the very hand that once had held him lovingly and guided him tenderly.

But unlike Abraham, who would allow none to watch this most private and painful moment, our heavenly Father permitted all to view that sacred scene atop Mt. Calvary where He sacrificed His only Son. There the Father invited both friend and foe—those who mourned and those who mocked—to witness the ratifying of this new covenant. This was something He did not permit when He established His first covenant with Israel, the giving of the Law through Moses.

At that time God had commanded they fence off Mt. Sinai so none might come near that holy mountain. But in instituting His new covenant—the grace that came through Jesus—God placed no barriers between man and the holy hill upon which He would sacrifice His sinless Lamb. On the contrary, He allowed not only Christ's followers to ascend Golgotha, but also His enemies. Disciples and detractors, angels and demons, all were invited to observe this sacred, sacrificial act. And if this was not enough, in the midst of Christ's sufferings the Father permitted His enemies to shame His holy Son through the curses of their lips and the spittle from their mouths. If ever heaven's hosts held their breath waiting for God's wrath to fall, it must have been at that moment.

Why would God ever allow men to view this sacred, hallowed act in such a profane and irreverent manner? Could not He, like Abraham, have taken His Son into the wilderness to present Him there as an offering for sin, a place where He could *privately* sacrifice Him for our redemption? Before ever going to the cross, Jesus knew full well what was prophesied of His public execution. He had read the Scriptures. Indeed, it was His foreknowledge of the horrors that awaited Him which caused Christ to cry, "Father, let this cup pass from Me. . . ."

Jesus fully understood that He was not only the Good Shepherd described in the twenty-third psalm, but also the Suffering Servant of the twenty-second. He, more than anyone else, realized that the hope and promise of the twenty-third psalm could never be fulfilled unless He suffered the painful and shameful death of the twenty-second psalm. As the Good Shepherd, He knew He must lay down His life for

His sheep if He were to take them safely "through the valley of the shadow of death." This He clearly taught in the 10th chapter of John's Gospel. "I am the good shepherd," He said. "The good shepherd lays down His life for the sheep. . . . I give them eternal life, and they shall never perish" (John 10:11–28).

Why would a loving Father allow His son to undergo such open mockery and public shame? Wasn't His death for our salvation enough? Must it also be turned into a public spectacle? For the answer to this we must go back to the fall of man as recorded in the book of Genesis.

The Serpent's temptation to Eve contained these words: "God knows that when you eat of it [the forbidden fruit] your eyes will be opened, and you will be like God" (Genesis 3:5). The deadly seed of doubt that Satan so craftily implanted in Eve's mind was this: "God does not have your best interests at heart. He only wants to keep you from reaching your fullest potential. The reason He has forbidden you to partake of this fruit stems from His own perverted desire to 'Lord it over you.' His own inflated ego prevents Him from allowing you to become like Him."

To digress for just a moment, I would like us to consider this satanic accusation against our Creator. First, in his temptation to Eve, Satan implied that God did not have her best interests at heart, otherwise He would not have withheld anything from her. This temptation, however, had not taken place within a vacuum but in the confines of Eden's perfect setting. All Eve would have had to do to rid her heart of any such doubts was merely look around at all the good things that God had given. But rather than looking to the bounty which her loving Creator had surrounded her with, she played into the devil's hands by focusing her attention on the one thing God had expressly forbidden—the fruit He had purposely placed in the center of the Garden to serve as a test of both her and Adam's loving obedience to Him.

Did we learn from their failure? I'm afraid not. Today many of us end up falling into that same trap by believing the Serpent's lying accusations. Though God has given us so much, it seems we quickly forget these blessings and focus entirely upon the forbidden fruit. As a result, we too fall prey to the big lie. It's so like the devil to make God out to be the thief and the liar when he himself has held that infamous distinction from the very beginning.

Another clear example of how Satan uses the big lie is found in the story of Balaam and Balak recorded in the book of Numbers. There Balak, king of Moab, tried unsuccessfully to get Balaam the seer to curse the advancing armies of Israel. But God would not allow him to curse His chosen ones. Each time Balaam began to speak, the Spirit of the Lord came upon him and he ended up blessing God's people rather than cursing them. Finally, after a third blessing was pronounced, Balak could no longer contain his anger: "I summoned you," he said, "to curse my enemies, but you have blessed them these three times. Now leave at once and go home! I said I would reward you handsomely, *but the Lord has kept you from being rewarded*" (Numbers 24:10–11).

That's exactly what Satan wants us to think today. He would have us believe that he's the rewarder and that God is the thief—that he would bless us while God would keep us from that blessing. Because Satan is the master deceiver, it's absolutely imperative that we never forget what James wrote under the Holy Spirit's inspiration: "Don't be deceived. . . . Every good and perfect gift is from above" (James 1:16–17). In other words, if God's not giving it, we don't want it! But how many of us have unnecessarily injured ourselves and others while hurting our heavenly Father by accepting some forbidden fruit from our Enemy's hand. Satan is like a perverted and twisted individual who would place in the hands of a young child a shiny new handgun. To the child it's an intriguing gift, but to the giver—a deadly trick.

Second, Satan tells Eve a bald-faced lie: God doesn't want you to be like Him. Now if, in fact, this was the case, why then did God declare, "Let us make man in our image, in our likeness" (Genesis 1:26)? Or was God just saying something that *sounded* noble but was meant only for the purpose of making "good reading" in the creation story? Obviously not! On the other hand, is it not likely that this divine pronouncement concerning man might indeed be the very reason why Satan so envies us and desires our destruction? For humans to be made in the image of God was our Creator's own plan, one which He devised long before we were ever formed. It is not something we proposed to Him after the fact.

To be made not only in God's image but into His likeness, however, was to involve more than just the initial act of our creation. It was to be a process begun by our Creator and continued on through our loving obedience to Him. What Satan argued was that we could have it all right now. We could instantaneously achieve our "divine destiny" if only we ignored the Word of God. But the truth of the matter was quite the opposite: Without the Word of the Lord guiding our every step, we would soon be stripped of life itself. Man was never meant to live by bread (or fruit) alone, "but by every word that proceeds from the mouth of God" (Deuteronomy 8:3 NKJV).

Satan's message of deception is still the same: "Only if you disregard God's Word can you truly be free—free to become 'as God,' making your own decisions about what is good and what is evil, what is right and what is wrong. You needn't depend on Him for your guidance in these matters. Be the master of your own destiny and the captain of your own ship!"

During the 1960's America began buying into this destructive philosophy. We started viewing God's Word as something archaic—something quite irrelevant for our progressive society. As a result we are now rapidly becoming a nation with little or no moral absolutes. As in Israel of old, "everyone does as he sees fit" (Judges 21:25). We are setting ourselves up as gods, each individual deciding what is right or wrong, good or evil. The result is the same as that which Israel suffered—moral and civil chaos.

In the beginning when man did choose to be the master of his own destiny and the captain of his own ship, all too soon he discovered that his destiny was death and his ship was sinking. Yet when all seemed hopeless—when man became enslaved by the very thing that promised him freedom—God sent the Living Word to dwell among us so that in His humanity Christ might regain for us what was lost in the Fall.

The image of God has been marred in each of us. As Paul states in Romans 3:23, we have all fallen "short of the glory of God." However, Jesus brought to us again the hope of glory restored. The primary work of the devil is to keep us from sharing in God's glory (i.e., the splendor of His nature and deeds), but our heavenly Father has other plans. Jesus Himself makes mention of this when He says, "Father . . . I have given them [My disciples] the glory that You gave Me" (John 17:22).

The end result of obedience to Christ, the Living Word, is the same as it was intended for us in the beginning. Now through Christ we are being fashioned into our Creator's likeness. In his second letter to the church at Corinth, Paul makes reference to this when he writes, "Now the Lord is the Spirit, and where the Spirit of the Lord is, there is freedom. And we, who with unveiled faces all reflect the Lord's glory, are being transformed into His likeness with ever-increasing glory, which comes from the Lord, who is the Spirit" (2 Corinthians 3:17–18).

Again in Romans 8:18, Paul speaks of "the glory that will be revealed in us" at the return of Christ. Notice he does not speak of the glory that will simply be revealed *to* us but the glory that will actually be revealed *in* us. God's glory is not just something we'll behold, but it's something we'll experience! Of this truth Paul joyously proclaimed: "...Christ in you, the hope of glory" (Colossians 1:27). At Jesus' second coming His glorious image will be fully stamped upon His own. John corroborates this in his first epistle when he writes, "What we will be has not yet been made known. But we know that when He appears *we shall be like Him,* for we shall see Him as He is. Everyone who has this hope in him purifies himself, just as He is pure" (1 John 3:2–3).

Here John boldly declares that everyone who walks in obedience to the Word of God, who "purifies himself," shall at Christ's return be brought into His glorious likeness. Then shall come to pass what God had always intended for man—that we be made into His likeness, that we be recipients of His glory. This was God's eternal purpose. Yet the path to Godlikeness has always been and shall always be *through* His eternal Word and never around it. Through humanity's disobedience to the Word of God, His glory within man quickly faded. But through our obedience to Christ, the Living Word, God is now giving back to us this lost glory in ever-increasing splendor.

Let's now return to the question of why God would have His Son publicly executed rather than privately sacrificed.

Why did He let the whole world mock this holy moment? After all, wouldn't Jesus' death still atone for our sins even if it were done privately? Of course it would. But when God gave His holy Lamb, He had more in mind than merely satisfying His own justice. The Father chose to crucify His Son before the eyes of the world so that He might forever silence those satanic voices that would call into question the sincerity of His love. Ever since the Fall it was this same evil accusation which God's enemies would constantly use to destroy mankind's trust in their Creator's goodness.

When our Adversary suggested that God had some sinister reason for commanding us not to eat of that one fruit, he was not only challenging our Creator's right of authority but he was also calling into question His love. And because he was able to successfully plant this insidious doubt in Eve's mind while she was yet in the midst of Paradise, how much easier, now that man is surrounded by the ills of Paradise lost, would it be for Satan to further seduce this fallen and weakened race? God realized the only way He could prove His love for us was through the public execution of His Son. He trusted that we would no longer doubt His love after witnessing the horrors of the Crucifixion.

Though God is our Creator, He is eternally bound by love to His creation. And though He is our sovereign Lord, in the midst of His sovereignty He erected a cross, and on that cross He had His heart's desire crucified. In this magnificent demonstration of His love, God let us clearly see that both His commands and His sovereignty are always and eternally guided by His love.

On the day Christ was crucified, God invited man to view the sacrifice that broke His heart. And in doing so, He did not limit its witnesses to just Christ's followers, but upon that very ground hallowed by the blood of the Lamb the

Father permitted both angels and apostles, demons and detractors to behold the horrors of the cross. Through the Crucifixion, God openly and painfully displayed His love for lost humanity. At last, that nagging question which had haunted the minds of men ever since the Fall—"Does God truly love us?"—was finally and forever settled. Indeed, the very spear that pierced the Savior's side would also drain the lifeblood from Satan's deadly lie!

Early in my Christian walk, the uncertainty of God's perfect love nearly destroyed my faith. In the winter of 1970 I recommitted my life to Christ. Though from preschool on I had regularly attended church with my mother and sister, at the age of seventeen I decided it was time to experience life in the "fast lane." A mere five years later found me as the defeated prodigal coming humbly back home to my heavenly Father, holding out to Him the pieces of my shattered life in hope He might find a way to put them back together again. Faithful to His nature, He tenderly began to mend each wound the Destroyer had inflicted.

But even in the midst of so much positive change within and without, there suddenly appeared on the horizon of my newfound faith a giant that seemed just as invincible as Goliath himself. And like that ancient reviler of Israel's army, morning by morning he came forth to challenge my faith and my God. But unlike Goliath, this "giant" seemed to have no Achilles heel. Try as I would, I was unable to strike the fatal blow. In fact, the giant I battled within actually grew larger and stronger as each day passed.

At first my enemy appeared as only a nagging question attacking the loving intentions of my Creator. But all too soon he became an ever-present threat to the very existence of my faith, for now this giant was brazenly assaulting the very character of God. "How can this One you serve be a

God of love," he taunted, "when the world He's created is filled with injustice . . . when sorrow and sufferings abound? How can a God of love allow such evil?"

His constant barrage began to take its toll upon my faith, and soon I found it quite impossible to trust my Creator. It was then I pleaded with God for some answer to this demon of doubt that was quickly destroying our relationship. I truthfully told Him that unless I received an answer to this tormenting question, I could only serve Him out of a sense of fear and not a heart of love; for how could I be devoted to One whom I could not trust?

It was into this dark pit of confusion that God sent a ray of light, and when it touched my troubled soul, I knew I would never again have to fight that giant. In the light of His truth God had answered any and every question that would ever again challenge His loving intentions. This liberating light of the Spirit came in the form of a question, followed by a brief directive.

The question, or should I say questions, which He clearly placed in my mind were these: "Do you believe I gave My Son to die for all? Do you believe what My Word declares when it says, 'For God so loved the world that He gave His only begotten Son that whosoever believes in Him should not perish but have everlasting life'?" "Yes, Lord," I quickly responded, "I do believe in the Crucifixion."

"Well then," He replied, "do you believe I could be so two-faced as to send My Son to die for mankind and yet at the same time be an unloving Creator who's untouched by human suffering?"

"No, Lord," I said. "I can't see how on the one hand You would sacrifice Your Son, while on the other be unconcerned about our sufferings."

Then He simply said, *"Trust My love."*

I knew I had my answer, and in a moment's time I was freed from the tormentor's snare—the giant lay dead, struck down by the Sword of Truth, slain by the Cross of Christ. Now when the evil one comes to question my Creator's love, I immediately march him back to the foot of the cross. And it's there I remind him that he himself knows this to be a fact since he was *there* the day God sacrificed His heart's desire, His only Son. Then I simply say, "Be gone, Satan, for it is written: 'This is how God showed His love among us: He sent His one and only Son into the world that we might live through Him. This is love: not that we loved God, but that He loved us and sent His Son as an atoning sacrifice for our sins'" (1 John 4:9–10).

6

"Father, Where Is the Lamb?"

$\mathcal{S}$ ensing something is wrong, a trusting, obedient son asks his loving father, "The fire and the wood are here, but where is the lamb for the burnt offering?" Because Abraham believes he must soon plunge the knife into Isaac's heart, this question fell like a dagger upon his own, inflicting its horrible pain into an already troubled heart. From the outset of the journey, Abraham knew his son would eventually ask this question, but only hoped it would be delayed as long as possible. Now he realizes Isaac is beginning to understand. In answering his son's question, Abraham unwittingly gives this prophetic response: "*God Himself will provide the lamb for the burnt offering, my son.*"

Just as from the start Isaac did not grasp the full extent of his father's mission nor the part that he would play in its fulfillment, neither did the boy Jesus. Scripture states that Jesus "grew in both stature and wisdom." The Bible does not tell us how old Jesus was when He first realized that He Himself was the sacrificial Lamb of which Abraham had spoken. Neither does it say just when or where it was that He first asked His Father this same question that Isaac had asked

Abraham. It might have been while He was listening to this very story being read in His synagogue at Nazareth, or possibly as He heard these words from the scroll of the prophet Isaiah:

> Surely He took up our infirmities and carried our sorrows, yet we considered Him stricken by God, smitten by Him, and afflicted. But He was pierced for our transgressions, He was crushed for our iniquities; the punishment that brought us peace was upon Him, and by His wounds we are healed. We all, like sheep, have gone astray, each of us has turned to his own way; and the Lord has laid on Him the iniquity of us all (Isaiah 53:4–6).

Again, we do not know exactly how or when it happened, but one day the boy Jesus came to realize that all men were under God's judgment for their sin. He knew from the words of Isaiah that, just like sheep, all men had gone astray. Each had turned to his own way and left the path of righteousness (Isaiah 53:6). He also knew that death was the judgment which God had pronounced upon sin, for the prophet Ezekiel had solemnly declared: "The soul that sins shall surely die" (Ezekiel 18:4). Through verses such as these, a young Jesus came to understand that if man was to ever escape God's judgment, a sacrifice must be offered in the people's place—a sacrificial lamb had to be slain.

He also knew that a mere animal sacrifice could never atone for man's sin, for the life of an animal was of far less value than that of a man. Justice could not be satisfied by substituting the life of a beast for one who was created in the image of God. And yet because there was no sinless man, there was none who could die for the sins of others. Each had to die for his own sins. Besides, Jesus knew that only unblemished sacrifices were acceptable to God; and, because all men were blemished by sin, this fact alone disqualified all from serving as the sacrificial lamb.

The moment the boy Jesus understood this truth was quite possibly the very hour that He too asked His Father, "Where is the lamb?" But unlike Abraham, God could not tell His Son that somehow, someway, the lamb would be provided. This Father had to say to His child, His only begotten, "You, My Son, are the Lamb." It was then that these words from the psalmist's pen took on new meaning for young Jesus: "Sacrifice and offering You did not desire, but a body You prepared for Me; with burnt offerings and sin offerings You were not pleased. Then I said, 'Here I am—it is written about Me in the scroll—I have come to do Your will, O God'" (Psalm 40:6–8). From this moment on both Father and Son moved resolutely toward that final hour when the prophetic words of Abraham would finally and painfully be fulfilled: "God Himself will provide the lamb"—an hour so dark and terrible that it would bring from the depths of Jesus' soul a cry of anguish that would pierce His Father's heart: "My God, My God, why have You forsaken Me?" (Mark 15:34).

Once Jesus realized His earthly destiny, certainly He must have begun searching the Holy Scriptures for those passages that would give Him further insight into the sacrificial death which awaited Him. And in this search, He would find the Twenty-second Psalm to be the most vivid and detailed foretelling of the Messiah's sufferings. In light of the cross, the Gospel writers themselves saw the particular significance of this psalm and drew from the riches of its prophetic words. In fact, as they witnessed the horrors of Christ's crucifixion, they heard with their own ears His tormented soul utter its opening cry, "My God, My God, why have You forsaken Me?" Through this prophetic psalm, Jesus knew the horrors of the cross long before He made His agonizing ascent up Calvary's hill.

In the Gospels, the story of the Crucifixion is told to us through the eyes of those who witnessed Christ's sufferings. But in the Twenty-second Psalm, we are given an insight into the very thought-life of Christ while He hung dying on the cross. Through its verses we catch a glimpse of the inner travail of His spirit as He bravely battled the malevolent powers of hell itself. More than any other passage of Scripture, this Davidic psalm predicted the sufferings of Christ. As king of Israel and prophet of God, David was a type or a foreshadow of the coming Messiah. This Jesus clearly understood.

From the opening words of this psalm—"*My God, My God, why have You forsaken Me?*"—we gain insight as to why, on the Day of Atonement, the high priest was to offer not one but two goats for the sins of Israel. Lots were cast to determine which of the two goats would be sacrificed to the Lord and which would be chosen as the "scapegoat" or the "goat of removal." The former goat was killed and its blood taken into the Most Holy Place. The latter was to "be presented alive before the Lord to be used for making atonement by sending it into the desert as a scapegoat" (Leviticus 16:10).

We know from Hebrews 9:12 that after Christ was crucified He entered heaven's Most Holy Place to present His blood for our eternal redemption. In this we see Christ fulfilling the prophetic picture represented by the first goat to be sacrificed on the Day of Atonement. But what of the "scapegoat" that was sent into the desert? Did Christ, likewise, fulfill the symbolism represented by this "goat of removal" that was also presented before the Lord? Of this goat, the Leviticus account says that Aaron was "to lay both hands on the head of the live goat and confess over it all the wickedness and rebellion of the Israelites—all their sins—and put them on the goat's head. He shall send the goat away into the desert. . . . The goat will carry on itself all their sins to a solitary place" (16:21–22).

This goat that had "all the wickedness and rebellion of the Israelites put on its head" was the one driven into a solitary, desert place. A place that I believe equates with the agony of Christ's soul when He cried, "My God, My God, why have You forsaken Me?" It is man's sin that will ultimately and eternally separate him from God. The prophet Isaiah proclaimed this when he said, "Your iniquities have separated you from your God" (Isaiah 59:2). Three times in Matthew's Gospel, Jesus describes final separation from God as being "thrown outside, into the darkness, where there will be weeping and gnashing of teeth" (8:12, 22:13, 25:30). I believe that just as Jesus had to fulfill the prophetic symbolism of the sacrificed goat, He would also need to fulfill the prophetic symbolism conveyed by the scapegoat. He, too, had to be driven out into a solitary land to experience the darkness and hopelessness of separation from God. In some real sense, Christ suffered the agony and torment of outer darkness—the essence of hell itself—when the Father placed on His Son's head the wickedness and rebellion of all mankind.

Never in all eternity had the Son been separated from the Father, nor the Father from the Son. Yet when Christ willingly bore the judgment of our sin upon Himself, He experienced for the first time the horrors and hopelessness of outer darkness. But because He was separated from the Father and driven away from His presence, *we* need never fear such a horrible fate. We may now rest assured that nothing in all creation "will be able to separate us from the love of God that is in Christ Jesus our Lord" (Romans 8:38–39).

From the very next verse of this Twenty-second Psalm,

"O My God, I cry out by day, but You do not answer, by night, and am not silent," we learn that the agony of the cross began days, even months before the actual crucifixion. Jesus did not begin His travail simply on the eve of His death. Luke confirms this when he records these words of Jesus spoken long before the day He was nailed to the cross: "I have a baptism to undergo, and how distressed I am until it is completed" (Luke 12:50). This baptism of which He spoke was the pouring out of His soul unto death.

Again Luke tells us that during the final week leading up to the cross, each evening Jesus would go up the Mount of Olives where He would spend the night. This was the very place where, on the night of His betrayal, He cried from the depths of His soul, "If it is possible, Father, let this cup pass from Me" (Luke 22:42). Luke tells us that such was the anguish of His heart that as He prayed, "His sweat was like drops of blood falling to the ground" (v. 44). Hebrews 5:7 describes it this way: "During the days of Jesus' life on earth, He offered up prayers and petitions with loud cries and tears to the One who could save Him from death." Because Jesus knew through the Scriptures what lay ahead of Him, the cross became His constant burden long before He fell beneath its load.

As we read further into this passage we find written these words: "But I am a worm and not a man, *scorned* by men and *despised* by the people. All who see Me mock Me; they hurl insults, shaking their heads" (Psalm 22:6–7). Early in His life Jesus learned of the shame and humiliation which lay ahead of Him, for it was clearly and painfully described in this psalm. Christ, the King of the universe—once clothed in splendor and enthroned on the praises of angels—would soon become an outcast of His own people, despised by men and stripped of any semblance of dignity. Yet He willingly bore this disgrace, for He knew that if *we* were to be clothed in His righteousness, then He must be stripped of His glory.

As we read on we are allowed to see into the realm of the spirit world, where we find the demons of darkness gathered at the foot of the cross and closing in for the kill: "Many bulls surround Me; strong bulls of Bashan encircle Me. Roaring lions tearing apart their prey open wide their mouths against Me" (22:12–13). The most important battle ever waged on this planet was not fought by the armies of the Egyptian, Babylonian, Greek, Roman or British empires. Rather, it was a battle fought by one solitary man as He stood against all the hosts of hell. There on Golgotha's hill, mankind's fate hung in the balance. There those evil spirits who once trembled in Christ's presence would now come to realize that He was at their mercy. The angels were no longer "given charge over Him, lest He should strike His foot against a stone" (see Matthew 4:6). Satan's legions knew they could now savagely attack Him without any fear of reprisal.

If ever there was a time and place where all demonic activity was centered, it must have been at the hour of our Lord's crucifixion on top Calvary's hill. Because Satan himself is a student of God's Word, the nether world of darkness knew full well that if Christ could be defeated, mankind's fate would forever be sealed. It was therefore imperative that they derail the work of Calvary.

As we look further into this chapter we find this description of the physical sufferings that would accompany the spiritual battle: "I am poured out like water, and all My bones are out of joint. My heart has turned to wax; it has melted away within Me. My strength is dried up like a potsherd, and My tongue sticks to the roof of My mouth; You lay Me in the dust of death" (vs. 14–15). Here it is clearly foretold that the sacrificial Lamb would suffer great *physical* pain as well as spiritual and mental anguish, for it was His Father's will. The prophet Isaiah confirms this when he writes: "Yet it was the Lord's will to crush Him and cause Him to *suffer* . . ." (Isaiah 53:10). "*He* has put Him to grief"(KJV).

Finally, through this prophetic psalm, Jesus learned just what form His physical sufferings would take: "They have pierced My hands and feet" (v. 16). He was well aware of the Roman mode of execution. Nailing the condemned to a cross was something He had most likely been an eyewitness to on at least one occasion. So it's a good possibility that He had seen firsthand the sufferings which awaited Him. We might then be quite certain that as He silently watched the horrors of a crucifixion, Satan did not allow this opportunity to pass him by. We may be assured that he was close at hand whispering in Jesus' ear that this, too, would be His own painful end if He did not go *his* way. "Remember," he might have said, "I promised I would give You the kingdoms of the world if You would but bow to my will. Play it smart, for if You continue on Your present course You, too, will experience the agony of a crucifixion. Consider carefully what You're doing. I want to place You on a throne. Your Father wants to put You on a cross."

So we see that through Scripture's prophetic account, Jesus bore the burden of the cross long before we nailed Him to it. And while on that cross, He suffered untold spiritual, mental, emotional and physical anguish so that through His completed sufferings we might gain total *victory*!

Finally, let's look again at the words of Hebrews 5:7: "During the days of Jesus' life on earth, He offered up prayers and petitions with loud cries and tears to the One who could save Him from death, *and He was heard because of His reverent submission*." But we must ask ourselves the question: When did God hear and when did God deliver? No loving father could ever turn a deaf ear to his own son's cry. So we may be certain that the Father immediately heard Jesus' cry. Yet even though He heard His cry, He delayed delivering Him until *after* Christ had completed the work the Father had given Him to do. It was only *in* death that the Son finished His Father's work and it was only *through* death that the Father delivered His Son. God did not abandon Jesus to the grave nor did He let His Holy One see decay (see Acts 2:27). On the third day the Father brought the Son back from the grave!

As followers of Christ, it would be good if we each remembered this principle. There will be times in our own lives that the Father's work for us will not be finished until we have gone to our own cross. Let's not falsely reason that just because we're undergoing sufferings, our heavenly Father has not heard our cries or seen our tears. Let's not err by assuming that God must immediately deliver us the moment we cry out. Though God is faithful to deliver, He will not do so before *His* appointed time and *our* completed mission.

7

Abraham Bound His Son and Laid Him on the Altar

As Abraham was binding his son in preparation for the sacrifice, his heart must have been breaking. And to make matters even more painful, as he bound his son, we find no indication that young Isaac made any attempt to free himself. Instead, he quietly yielded to his father's will. As it was with Isaac, so it was with Christ. "He was led like a lamb to the slaughter, and as a sheep before her shearers is silent, so He did not open His mouth" (Isaiah 53:7). Just like Isaac, Jesus would not resist His Father's will. He, too, would obediently surrender to His eternal purpose.

When the Scriptures tell us that the soldiers bound Jesus and led Him away (see John 18:12), they were able to do so only because He had already been bound by the will of His Father. Jesus knew for certain that this *was* His Father's will and this was the hour of its implementation; for as the soldiers drew near to bind Him, He said to His disciples, "Shall I not drink the cup the Father has given Me?" (John 18:11). The Father had given Him that cup just moments earlier. Immediately after crying out, "Father, if You are willing, take this cup from Me; yet not My will, but Yours be done" (Luke 22:42), it's recorded that an angel was sent to strengthen Him. Jesus clearly understood this response from the Father. He needed no further instructions. The long-awaited hour had come; there would be no delay and there would be no deliverance.

The Father had sent an angel to minister to His Son this one last time before all the angels would have to help-lessly stand by and watch the *Author of Life* quietly surrender to death. Jesus knew that the words the prophet Isaiah had penned were written for this very hour and this very pur-pose: "It was the Lord's will to crush Him and cause Him to suffer" (Isaiah 53:10).

In his account of Christ's arrest (John 18:4–5) John records that as the guards drew near, Jesus asks them, "Who is it you want?" They reply, "Jesus of Nazareth." In identify-ing Himself, He responds—"*I Am.*" In a prior passage, puzzled skeptics had asked Christ who He thought He was, for He had just claimed He'd been around since Abraham's time. In answer to their question Jesus declared, "Before Abraham was born, *I Am*" (John 8:58). At this the Jews wanted to stone Him, for they knew He was claiming to be the very One who'd spoken to Moses at Horeb from the midst of the burning bush—the One who declared His name to be the eternal *I Am* (Exodus 3:14).

Once again Jesus makes this same claim to those who had come to arrest Him. When they said, "We are looking for Jesus of Nazareth," His response was simply, "*I Am.*" And at this pronouncement, John says in verse 6, "they drew back and fell to the ground." There was such power in this decla-ration that no foe could stand in His presence. So one last time before they led Him away, Christ offered them powerful proof that He was indeed the Son of the Living God—the eternal *I Am*—in both declaration and demonstration.

At this point Peter got really brave, took up a sword, and struck the high priest's servant. He must have reasoned that there was no chance of being defeated since Jesus had just laid low several men with only the *spoken word*! Immediately, however, Christ rebuked Peter, reminding both him and his fellow disciples that He must obey the Father and "drink the cup He had been given." Then He explained to Peter just how foolish his attempt at helping had been. "Do you think I cannot call on My Father," He said, "and He will at once put at My disposal more than twelve legions of angels?" (Matthew 26:53). That would have meant a minimum of one legion for Himself and one for each of the remaining eleven disciples—certainly sufficient firepower (a Roman legion had 6,000 soldiers) to destroy not only those who had come to arrest Him but the entire Roman empire as well!

Consider now the obedience and self-discipline Christ displayed at that moment. It's difficult enough to endure any type of suffering, but especially unjust suffering. Now imagine adding to that unjust suffering the knowledge that you can escape from it at will. This makes remaining under such unwarranted suffering nearly impossible. This was the situation in which Christ was placed. Possibly Jesus' greatest temptation came at that moment. As we've already noted, He was well aware of the tremendous physical, emotional and spiritual pain the next few hours would bring. Christ would now have to draw from the inner strength of His character to keep from beckoning the armies of heaven to come and set Him free. Though with just a word Jesus could have worked His own deliverance, He did not. As followers of Christ, the lesson for us is clear: Though at times we might be tempted to deliver ourselves, we must never do so if it means stepping off the path of obedience. Rather, in obedience, we must "take up our cross and follow Him."

As we consider the remarkable restraint that Christ exhibited, we must not forget the Father's role in this extraordinary and crucial victory. The Father had brought His Son to the cross neither unprepared nor prematurely. He had carefully taken His Son through the rigors and disciplines of life, and now was confident that Jesus was ready to face His darkest and most difficult hour. He was certain that these disciplines had formed in His Son the strength of character that was absolutely essential if He hoped to be victorious in this His final battle . . . a battle that would ultimately determine the fate of all mankind. If Jesus had been coddled and pampered by the Father, He would not have been able to endure this most painful hour—which would have left us to perish in our sin.

From the humble beginnings of Jesus' birth and early childhood, to His forty days of fasting in the wilderness, to the constant and exhausting demands of ministry, the Father had carefully honed the Son's spiritual, emotional and mental makeup. Now just as it would be utterly foolhardy to attempt to run a marathon without having first built up one's physical and mental stamina, in this case it would have literally meant spiritual suicide for both Christ and mankind if He had gone to the cross untrained and untested. Without the Father's deliberate and diligent training, the Son would have failed to complete His ultimate "marathon."

It's right for us to conclude, then, that past hardships are absolutely necessary for present victories. But it seems the Church has forgotten this principle. The Body of Christ is filled with those who would ask God to do great things through their lives while expecting it to happen with little or no hardships along the way. Remember, Scripture states that it is not simply our *faith* that works within us the endurance that perfects our character, but it is the *testing* of our faith that accomplishes this good work. That's why we are to rejoice in the face of adversity—not because we enjoy the pain or the struggle but because we know that without these, Christlike character can never be formed. And without this Christlike character we will forever be "coming down off the cross," thwarting the Father's plan.

Let's then recall what Scripture teaches concerning the necessity of suffering and how it related to Christ Himself: "Though He was a son He learned obedience from what He suffered and, once made perfect, He became the source of eternal salvation for all who obey Him" (Hebrews 5:8). The word that's been translated in this verse as "perfect" comes from the same Greek word translated "mature" in the passage cited earlier: "Consider it pure joy, my brothers, whenever you face trials of many kinds, because you know that the testing of your faith develops perseverance. Perseverance must finish its work so that you may be *mature* and complete, not lacking anything" (James 1:2–4).

God has made it quite clear that the *path* to Christian maturity—to being perfected—is never one of ease. Indeed, without adversity we'll forever be running from the cross, never developing the endurance necessary to finish the race. Before we can be bound by the Father's will and taken to our own cross, we must first be successful in the lesser trials so we might gain the inner strength that's necessary for our *remaining* on the cross.

Finally, we must not think of the cross as an end in itself. It's only a necessary step that must be taken before there can be a resurrection! Jesus did not focus on the cross. If He had done that, He would have undoubtedly failed. Look where the writer of Hebrews says Christ placed His focus: ". . . For the *joy set before Him* [Jesus] endured the cross, scorning its shame, and sat down at the right hand of the throne of God" (Hebrews 12:2).

Jesus focused on "the joy set before Him," not on the sufferings of Calvary. And just what was the joy that was set before Christ? It was not simply the joy of resurrection; rather, it was the hope of gaining a bride for Himself! We were His focus. We were His source of joy—not the momentary sufferings of the cross nor even the promise of resurrection morning. Every triumphant Christian—every believer who hopes to persevere—must be like-minded. Indeed, the writer of Hebrews tells us where we, too, must place our focus: "Let us run with perseverance the race marked out for us. Let us fix our eyes on Jesus . . ." (vs. 1–2). And who is this Jesus on whom we are to fix our gaze? He is the fairest of all bridegrooms, who has prepared for us the unbounded joys of His eternal kingdom. He willingly sacrificed Himself to gain our love by His atoning death. If we fail to focus our hopes and dreams upon this supreme Lover of our souls, then we will have neglected our greatest source of strength and inspiration.

From the pages of ancient history we find a story that beautifully illustrates the love that Christ has shown for us and, in turn, the way that we're to respond to Him:

> After an important victory, Cyrus, king of Persia, took prisoner a noble prince with his wife and children, to whom the king said, "What will you give me to set you at liberty?"
>
> The prince replied, "Half of all I possess."
>
> King Cyrus continued, "And what if I release your children?"
>
> "Then I will give all I possess," the prince quickly responded.
>
> Thinking he had nothing left to give, Cyrus then

said, "But what if I should set your wife at liberty? What then will you give me?"

"Then, my lord," replied the prince, "I will lay down my life"

Won by the true nobility of the man, Cyrus immediately set them at liberty without any recompense whatsoever. That evening, when the prince and his wife were rejoicing together over their new-found freedom, he said, "Did you not think Cyrus a handsome man?"

She replied, "I didn't notice him sufficiently well to tell."

Puzzled by her answer, the prince inquired, "How could you have not noticed?"

"I did not notice," she answered, "for my eyes were fixed on him who said he would lay down his life for me."

If we, too, will learn to fix our eyes on the One who loves us best—the One who laid down His life for ours—it will help safeguard us against all destructive and distractive forces that would draw us away from our only true source of eternal life and love.

8

Abraham . . . Took the Knife to Slay His Son

*A*braham was not testing God, God was testing
Abraham. Abraham wasn't just waiting to see how far the
Lord would have him go before stopping him, but when he
raised the knife, he did so with the full intent of plunging it
into Isaac's heart and thus into his own. In lifting the knife,
Abraham was not merely performing an outward religious
act with no accompanying inward commitment; but when
he'd told his servants to wait behind while he and his son
would ascend the mountain and there *worship* God, Abraham
had meant what he had said. He dared not approach God
insincerely, but would faithfully offer Him the honor due His
name—worship given "in spirit and in truth."

To do this, Abraham knew he must be willing to finish
by deed what he had purposed in heart. He knew that if he
were not willing to complete what he had begun, all he had
done up to that point would have been in vain, for worship
is unacceptable if obedience is incomplete. And unless we,
like Abraham, truly intend to bring the knife down upon
that which God has asked us to surrender, all we may have

done in preparation for that sacrifice is nothing more than vain religious trappings, notwithstanding our good intentions or declarations of faith.

James argues this very point when he says that our faith is useless unless it is accompanied by action. He then proceeds to illustrate his point by using this sacrifice of Isaac: "You foolish man, do you want evidence that faith without deeds is useless? Was not our ancestor Abraham considered righteous for what he did when he offered his son Isaac on the altar?" (James 2:20-21). Although Abraham's righteousness, as Paul wrote, was imputed to him because of his faith (Romans 4:9), James adds that his faith was evidenced through his deeds: "As the body is dead without the spirit, so faith without deeds is dead" (James 2:26). Because it is impossible to please a living God with a dead faith, whatever we purpose in heart, we must be willing to perform in deed.

At this juncture it's also important to mention that the testing of Abraham was not complete until the intentions of Abraham were certain. Notice how James speaks as if Abraham had in fact accomplished the sacrifice: "He offered his son Isaac on the altar." Only at the point where Abraham was actually going to bring down the knife on Isaac could God stay the hand of His obedient servant. It wasn't until this very moment that his faith could be shown to be complete through his actions. And it was only then that God was free to declare, "It is enough. Now I know."

Keil and Delitzsch in their *Commentary on the Old Testament* wrote the following:

> In this eventful moment the Lord called down from heaven to Abraham to stop . . . [for] the sacrifice was already accomplished in his heart, and he had fully satisfied the requirements of God. . . . God did not desire the sacrifice of Isaac by slaying and burning him upon the altar, but Abraham's complete surrender, and *will-*

ingness to offer him up to God even by death. Nevertheless, the divine command was given in such a form, that
Abraham could not understand it in any other way than
as requiring an outward burnt-offering, because there
was no other way in which Abraham could accomplish
the complete surrender of Isaac, than by an actual preparation for really offering the desired sacrifice.

Have we displayed like faith? Have we shown such sincerity in our worship? Perhaps we have had the best of intentions as we eagerly began our personal journey to our own
Moriah. Perhaps we resolutely ascended the mountain of sacrifice and, once there, even took hold of the knife. But if we
fell short in our obedience by refusing to lift that knife above
our most prized treasure—with the full intent of bringing it
down—then in truth we have given nothing and we have
gained nothing!

To cite another biblical example of one who successfully
completed her sacrificial act, let us consider Ruth. Here was
a childless widow who—for the love of her mother-in-law,
Naomi, and Naomi's God—was willing to bring down the
knife on her hopes of ever having a husband and a family.
Through faith and love she surrendered her future plans and
dreams, to follow after a destitute old woman who had lost
everything this world deems of value. Yet in her sacrifice,
her faith touched the heart of God. By her seemingly foolish
act it appeared to the world that Ruth had just plunged a
knife into the heart of her future happiness. Even in her
mother-in-law's eyes she was acting foolishly. "Return home,"
Naomi said. "Why would you come with me? . . . I am too
old to have another husband. Even if I thought there was
still hope for me—even if I had a husband tonight and then
gave birth to sons—would you wait until they grew up? Would
you remain unmarried for them?" (Ruth 1:11–13). Yet in
heaven's eyes, she had just sacrificed the very thing that

would have kept her from receiving the blessings God had prepared for her while yet in her mother's womb!

If Ruth had not shown such sacrificial faith, she would never have known what might have been—for God's Word tells us that she not only gained a husband of character and wealth, but through her we trace the lineage of Christ! I believe that on the Day of Judgment the saddest moment of all might just possibly be when God reveals the things that could have been—things which He had prepared for our good and His glory. But because we were unwilling to make the sacrifice, we failed to gain the very blessings which our heavenly Father had planned for us before the dawn of time.

In reading the biblical accounts of those who made such sacrifices, we must not forget that these people wrestled with the same weaknesses which beset our lives. We must not think they were exempt from struggling with human frailty. It was not any easier for them than it is for us to make these sacrifices. In doing what they did, they too had to go against all that appeared reasonable. In those times when they found that human logic conflicted with God's demands, they refused to allow it to paralyze their faith. Through faith, they were able to do what appeared most unreasonable.

But it's in these times of conflict that we often forget that, though we have a reasonable faith, we also have a God who transcends human reasoning—a God who declares, "My thoughts are not your thoughts, neither are your ways My ways. . . . As the heavens are higher than the earth, so are My ways higher than your ways and My thoughts than your thoughts" (Isaiah 55:8–9). Therefore, let not logic betray faith nor reason forbid obedience. If God should so command, let us also with that same Abrahamic faith raise the sacrificial knife to make ready its thrust into the heart of that which is most precious to us.

In my own life I've experienced both victory and defeat in those moments when my faith and reason were at odds. But since it's always easier to share our triumphs rather than our failures, I'll take the easy way out and tell you about one of those times I did succeed.

Even though this is a story that ultimately ends in victory, it certainly didn't start that way. It begins on the day I was asked to resign my position as youth pastor. Because this was my first full-time staff position at any church, it was especially difficult for me to hear these unexpected words from my senior pastor: "Things aren't working out as well as we'd hoped. I think it best that you begin looking for a new position."

I know the first question each reader would like answered before we go any further: "Why?" Well, I'm happy to report that the reason I was asked to leave had nothing to do with either a moral failure on my part or some other blemish on my personal integrity. The fact of the matter was that I did not make the best of youth pastors.

But in the midst of this disappointing and discouraging time for both my wife and me, God was faithful to share with us a word of hope and promise. Yet because it came from an unusual source in an unusual way, we could have easily ignored it—especially since we were listening for the sound of thunder while God chose to use something a little less ostentatious. He had elected to speak to us through an elderly lady whom I couldn't remember ever meeting, although her sister—through whom this message was relayed—assured us we had. On top of this unusual delivery system, the verses of Scripture which the sister was asked to pass along to us seemed so inappropriate at the time. They were taken from the end of Paul's first letter to the church at Corinth and served as some parting instructions about an upcoming visit that young

Timothy would soon be paying them. "If Timothy comes," Paul wrote, "see to it that he has nothing to fear while he is with you, for he is carrying on the work of the Lord, just as I am. No one, then, should refuse to accept him. Send him on his way in peace so that he may return to me. I am expecting him along with the brothers" (1 Corinthians 16:10–11).

When this older saint called her sister to relay this message to us, she simply said that during her devotions that morning the Lord had impressed upon her to pass these two verses along to John. She went on to say that she'd received nothing more than this distinct impression and that she hadn't the vaguest clue as to what all this meant. Well, I must say that when I read these verses, I was somewhat disappointed. I'd been hoping for something much more direct and certainly something much more understandable. But the woman assured us that this was something she had never seen her sister do before, so it must have been something she felt very strongly about.

All we could do was try and make some sense out of what had been passed along, hoping that it was indeed from the Lord. Besides, by this time we were pretty desperate— we'd latch on to anything! So the more we prayerfully considered this, the more we were persuaded that if there was any meaning for us at all in these verses, it must have meant that we would be going back to what we would consider our home base. We came to this conclusion because of Paul's instruction to send Timothy on his way back to him: he was "*expecting to see him* along with the brothers."

A little over a year later that word seemed ready to come to pass, for the very church in which we were married and had later served as volunteer youth workers called to tell us that their pastor had just resigned and they would like us to come and speak with their pulpit committee. We could hardly believe our ears! God was bringing about what He'd spoken to us through a forgotten sister who'd sent such an unusual message.

At the time the call came, we were located in a very small community pastoring a very small church. And although we had adjusted quite well to rural life and had truly come to love and enjoy our flock, we felt we wanted somewhat more of a challenge. Besides, since this was a promise from the Lord that was about to be fulfilled before our very eyes—or so we thought—we were quite excited to begin this new phase of our ministry in this promised position.

As it happened, however, when we went to interview with the pulpit committee, one gentleman asked if we would feel comfortable accepting the position if we received only a 2/3rds vote from the body. Now in the denomination in which we serve, each local body is autonomous, electing its own pastor through its membership. Their church by-laws stated that to be elected, a candidate must receive at least 2/3rds of the votes cast by the membership. Not wanting to appear overconfident—even though I knew God was putting all this together—I quickly responded that I wouldn't come on just a 2/3rds vote. I told them I would like a stronger base of support.

I think you can guess what happened next. They did invite me to come and speak to the body. We accepted, and after the Sunday evening service the membership was asked to cast their ballots. We got *exactly* 2/3rds of the votes cast! After returning to our present church we were feeling like those who had voted against our coming had botched God's plans—that the will of man and not the will of God had prevailed. In our hurt and disappointment we reasoned that since there existed no scriptural precedent for selecting church leadership through the democratic process, this unbiblical method was hindering the fulfillment of God's promise for our lives and that congregation.

A few days later we received a phone call from the presbyter of that particular section informing us that the man who had asked whether or not we would come on a minimum vote had posed that question with an ulterior motive. He had a friend whom he wanted to be the new pastor and was attempting to sway the church to his way of thinking. So the presbyter told me that as far as he was concerned, the church was ours. I told him I needed time to think it over and would call him back.

After hanging up the phone I immediately got down on my knees to pray. As soon as I began to ask God for His guidance, the Holy Spirit brought these verses to my mind from Psalm 15: "Lord, who may dwell in Your sanctuary? Who may live on Your holy hill? He whose walk is blameless and who does what is righteous, who speaks the truth from his heart . . . *who keeps his oath even when it hurts.*"

I had my answer. Even though I felt God had given me a word concerning returning to that church, I knew that He had now told me I must not violate His Word to insure its fulfillment. And even though this phone call from the sectional presbyter had given me a logical reason for accepting this new position, I knew I must not place reason above faith. If God had truly promised this, then He would bring it to pass without transgressing any other part of His Word. Furthermore, since I knew that the Scriptures teach that God is both omniscient and omnipotent, I had to believe that because He had foreseen the outcome of the vote, in one way or another He could have also changed the outcome. So I called the presbyter back and told him that I could not accept the position. Even though it hurt—even though I felt as though I was sacrificing the very thing that

God had promised—I knew I had made the right choice. The moment I hung up the phone, it was as though a tremendous weight had been lifted from my spirit.

One year later the same congregation called me back to meet once more with their pulpit committee, as the church was going through some difficult times and the pastor they had elected was now leaving for another position. Again I spoke at the church, but this time with a dramatically different outcome. Of all the votes cast, only two came back against our election. As I reflected on what had happened, I realized I had forgotten what God had impressed upon my heart immediately following our termination as youth pastors. It was from Psalm 138 and had come as a reassuring word in a time when we were so uncertain about our future: "Though I walk in the midst of trouble, You preserve my life. . . . *The Lord will fulfill His purpose for me*; Your love, O Lord, endures forever" (vs. 7–8). In all of this I learned that the promises of God are just that—His to give and His to *fulfill*. Whatever God has purposed for the lives of His own, He will make certain it comes to pass—provided that we trust His heart even when we can't trace His hand!

God had promised Abraham that He would make him the father of a multitude, but now He was asking him to do the unthinkable . . . to thrust a knife into the heart of his sole heir, the very one on whom the promise rested. Yet again, because it was God's promise to give, it was also His to fulfill—and to fulfill in whatever manner or method He might choose.

Though we have focused our attention in this chapter primarily on the instrument of death (i.e., the knife) that Abraham had taken up the mountain, we must not forget that he also took with him the instruments for completing his sacrificial act. After he had plunged the knife into Isaac's heart, he would be required to burn the body. Thus, he had Isaac himself carry the wood up Moriah while he took the fire and the knife.

Here's what Calvin wrote of this tremendous act of faith and obedience: "Abraham did not bind the power of God to the life of Isaac but was persuaded that it would be no less effective in his ashes when he was dead than when he was alive and breathing." What an incredible faith! Abraham believed that God was able to fulfill His promise through Isaac even if his body was turned to ashes! Remember, he had just told his servants, "Stay here with the donkey while I and the boy go over there. We will worship and then we will come back to you."

Abraham had already lived the faith that Paul would write of some 2,000 years later: "This happened that we might not rely on ourselves but on God, *who raises the dead*" (2 Corinthians 1:9). And so the writer of Hebrews speaks in this manner of Abraham's sacrifice: "By faith Abraham, when God tested him, offered Isaac as a sacrifice. He who had received the promises was about to sacrifice his one and only son, even though God had said to him, 'It is through Isaac that your offspring will be reckoned.' Abraham reasoned that God could raise the dead, and figuratively speaking, he did receive Isaac back from death" (Hebrews 11:17–19).

If we believe in the God of Abraham, then we must be confident that He can do as much with the *ashes* of His promises as He can with the *embodiment* of them. Since this is indeed the case, we mustn't think it strange if God should allow our hopes to be sacrificed on the altar of our obedience. For it is from the ashes of our surrendered hope that He will often resurrect the fulfillment of His promise!

9

"Now I Know That You Fear God"

As Abraham was about to bring down the knife, the angel of the Lord called out to him, "Abraham! Abraham! Do not lay a hand on the boy. Do not do anything to him. Now I know that you fear God, because you have not withheld from Me your son, your only son." Abraham's hand was stayed . . . Isaac was not slain. This father did not have to undergo the untold agony of killing his only son. He was spared the heartbreak of watching his beloved die at his own hands.

How unlike, though, our heavenly Father who was not spared this pain. He did indeed bring down the knife upon His only Son so that we might live and not die. And even though in our wickedness we cried out for Christ's blood, man alone could not and did not kill Jesus. We only served as the instrument of death which the Father chose to slay His Son. . . . We were the knife He held in His hand.

On the day of Pentecost Peter acknowledges this truth when he says, "This man [Jesus] was handed over to you by God's set purpose and foreknowledge" (Acts 2:23). The prophet Isaiah also made a similar declaration, although his pronouncement was made nearly 700 years prior to the actual crucifixion: "He had done no violence, and there was no deceit in His mouth. Yet it was the will of the Lord to bruise Him; *He has put Him to grief*" (Isaiah 53:9–10 RSV). And as we read again the prophetic words of Psalm 22, we also find this statement confirming the Father's role in the death of His Son: "My strength is dried up like a potsherd, and My tongue sticks to the roof of My mouth; *You* [God] *lay Me in the dust of death*" (v. 15).

Jesus died at the hands of His Father. He was the "Lamb that was slain from the foundation of the world." The Father Himself had caused the knife to pierce His own Son's heart, and when that knife had found its mark, a bruised and bleeding Son drew His final breath and cried, "*It is finished!*" while horrified angels bowed their heads in holy silence and a grief-stricken Father closed tear-filled eyes and wept alone.

In light of such love we are compelled to confess, "Now I know that You love me, God, for You have not withheld from me Your Son, Your only Son." The Apostle Paul shares this astounding and comforting truth when he writes these words to the church at Rome: "He who did not spare His own Son, but gave Him up for us all—how will He not also, along with Him, graciously give us all things?" (Romans 8:32). Paul rightly reasons that since God sacrificed what was most precious to Him, there can remain little doubt as to His loving intentions towards all. In the 17th chapter of John's Gospel Jesus reaffirms the magnitude of the Father's love for us when He prays, "May they [Christians] be brought to complete unity to let the world know that You sent Me *and have loved them even as You loved Me*" (v. 23).

Can it be that the Father does love us even as He loves His only begotten Son? Dare we think such a thing? Indeed, for God's Word tells us time and again that we truly are His children, even to the point of being named "co-heirs with Christ." Consider, for example, these words which Jesus shares with one of the women who had come to anoint His body on the morning of the resurrection: "Do not hold on to Me, for I have not yet returned to the Father. Go instead to My brothers and tell them 'I am returning to My Father and *your Father*'" (John 20:17). Then in his first epistle to the church, John writes these powerful and promise-filled words: "How great is the love the Father has lavished on us, that we should be called children of God! *And that is what we are!*" (1 John 3:1).

In truth the Father has lavished His love upon us by bringing us into this special relationship with Him. We are all well aware of the fact that children occupy a privileged place in the hearts of their fathers. As a pastor, a friend, a neighbor and an acquaintance, many people in this world can call out my name and I will respond to them by virtue of our relationship. But there are only two people among the billions that inhabit this planet that can address me as *father*—and these two know they hold a special place in my heart. Therefore, they will boldly ask of me things that others dare not. And they will ask with the full assurance that I will respond to their needs and desires. That's how it is with our heavenly Father. In Christ Jesus we are truly sons and daughters of the Most High. And on the basis of that relationship we can confidently and expectantly pray, "*Our Father. . . .*"

It's so important to remember that when Christ taught us to pray, He began by that simple declaration, "*Our Father.*" He could have said, "O eternal God, Creator of heaven and earth, hear the prayer of Your humble servants. . . ." But He did not, for He wanted us to always remember that through Him we have been given the right of *sonship*. Again John writes, "Yet to all who received Him [Christ], to those who believed in His name, He gave the right to become *children of God*" (John 1:12). And again Jesus tells His disciples in the 16th chapter of this same Gospel, "In that day you will ask in My name. I am not saying that I will ask the Father on your behalf: No, the Father Himself loves you because you have loved Me" (John 16:26–27).

In my own life it wasn't until several years after becoming a Christian that I first began to truly understand the significance of this marvelous truth. Oh, I knew what Scripture said about Christians being children of God, but it was something that had never really impacted my spirit . . . that is, not until one of the darkest days of my ministry.

I had gone into prayer that morning feeling as though I might never fully recover from what had happened the night before. It was the evening of our annual church business meeting and things had not gone well at all. Now for you who have been through these meetings, you might be thinking, "Hey, what's the big deal? Aren't they all just one gigantic headache?" Well, this one was more than just a huge headache, it was a major migraine; for somewhere in the middle of that meeting, I had been accused of authorizing the spending of $25,000 without the approval of the church board. That was a serious charge!

What made matters even worse was that after going home for the evening, feeling as though my personal integrity had just been destroyed, one board member—who would not speak up during the discussion that night—called to assure me that he'd remembered them approving this expenditure. But of what help was that when the entire membership had heard and thought differently? I knew he felt badly, but why hadn't he spoken up in the meeting?

So as I began my prayer time the following morning, I

was seriously considering resigning as pastor and looking for any type of employment that would get me far away from church leadership. But in this moment of pain and darkness the Father began to open my eyes to the relationship I had had with Him since the first day of my conversion, but never had truly understood nor appreciated. This revelation began unfolding as I desperately cried *"Father"* over and over again. And as I continued to cry out *"Father,"* He gently reminded me that this was exactly who He was . . . my Father. And because He was my Father, I suddenly began to realize that I didn't have to do everything right for Him to love me, nor did I have to perform perfectly for Him to care. He loved me because of a *relationship*, not because of some grand or flawless *performance* on my part.

As I continued to call upon my Father with this new-found awareness, He reminded me that this was exactly what Christ Himself had done as He agonized in Gethsemane. As Jesus travailed in prayer on that night of His betrayal, the cry from His heart began with *"Abba, Father!"* Immediately I remembered the words of Paul found in the 8th chapter of Romans: "For you did not receive a spirit that makes you a slave again to fear, but you received the Spirit of sonship. And by Him we cry 'Abba, Father'" (v. 15).

Though nothing had changed that morning as far as my circumstances, everything had changed within me! And as this truth of the Father's love began to flood my soul, I knew that everything was going to be all right. If God, my heavenly Father, was for me, who then could be against me? Even before this issue had come before the membership, my omniscient heavenly Father had already made provision for its peaceful resolution. And let me quickly add that these charges were not made out of malice, for with the exception of the previously mentioned board member, they all honestly believed I had gone ahead and acted without their consent.

It just so happened that at the board meeting where the decision to spend this money was made, the secretary had been absent. So instead of someone taking notes that evening, we had taped the entire session. This was not the normal procedure. In fact, it was the *only* time we had ever done this. When the tapes were played back, the two members who had insisted most strongly that I had indeed proceeded without their consent were the same two who were heard most clearly *giving* their consent.

Looking back over the entire situation, I can honestly thank God for that misunderstanding, for even though at the time it hurt so deeply, without it happening I don't know when I would have come to realize that God was indeed my heavenly Father. But now through the revelation of this truth I knew I had the power to touch His heart and influence His decisions. I had discovered that I was not just another of His creatures . . . I was indeed *His child!* Now when I lift my voice and cry *"Father,"* I have no doubt whatsoever that His ear is attentive to my plea.

Listen to how the psalmist describes this remarkable influence we have with our Creator: "In my distress I called to the Lord; I cried to my God for help. From His temple He heard *my* voice; *my* cry came before Him, *into His ears*" (Psalm 18:6). Note how the psalmist says that God singled out his cry from all other voices in heaven and earth. Although there is a continual flow of praise and prayer ascending before God's throne, He still hears each solitary cry. Surely there is a place in God's heart for every one of His blood-bought children . . . a place no one else can occupy but those whose names are inscribed therein.

Before ending this chapter, I know I would be remiss if I did not address one other aspect of our heavenly Father's love—one that's often ignored or simply overlooked: *discipline*. Listen carefully to what the writer of Hebrews says about the link between love and discipline:

> My son, do not make light of the Lord's discipline, and do not lose heart when He rebukes you, because the Lord disciplines those He loves, and He punishes everyone He accepts as a son. Endure hardship as discipline; God is treating you as sons. For what son is not disciplined by his father? If you are not disciplined (and everyone undergoes discipline), then you are illegitimate children and not true sons. Moreover, we have all had human fathers who disciplined us and we respected them for it. How much more should we submit to the Father of our spirits and live! Our fathers disciplined us for a little while as they thought best; but God disciplines us for our good, that we may share in His holiness. No discipline seems pleasant at the time, but painful. Later on, however, it produces a harvest of righteousness and peace for those who have been trained by it (Hebrews 12:5–11).

Notice that the writer uses the word discipline (or some form thereof) *TEN* different times in this brief exhortation. Obviously he doesn't want us to miss the point: i.e., love and discipline are inseparable.

For our purposes I wish to take special note of just two statements included in this passage:

1) *"Do not lose heart when He rebukes you, because the Lord disciplines those He loves."*

2) *"No discipline seems pleasant at the time, but painful."*

As we've already stated, Satan's primary goal is to drive a wedge between us and our Creator, and his primary means is to bring us to a place where we question the purity and/or wisdom of God's love. So Satan will use those times when our heavenly Father is disciplining us as opportunities to achieve his ill purposes. He is forever trying to thwart the Father's plan in the discipline of His children and turn it for evil. Rather than having God's children respond correctly and repent, Satan wants them to become either disheartened and give up or resentful and rebel. This is what the writer means when he says, "Do not lose heart when He rebukes you." Each time our heavenly Father chastens us, Satan is right there to "pour salt into the wound." The author of Hebrews takes his quote from Proverbs 3:11 where the wording is somewhat stronger: "My son, do not *despise* the Lord's discipline and do not *resent* His rebuke." In the process of writing this book I personally experienced how chastening can lead to despair and despair to resentment. For me this was quite a shock, for I've always considered myself to be a rather upbeat person.

Somewhere in the middle of the writing of this book I had gone to the mountains to spend some time in fasting and prayer. At the time I was facing some problems with staff relationships and felt I needed some direction on what or what not to do. When I arrived at the campground, the director's wife gave me a tape of worship choruses that she felt would be of benefit to me during my stay there. I now unquestionably believe that she was led of the Lord to give me this tape.

There was one particular song by Lynn DeShazo that became the cry of my heart for the next three days. I played it and *prayed* it over and over again. These are its lyrics:

Turn my heart, O Lord, like rivers of water; turn my
    heart, O Lord, by Your hand,
Till my whole life flows in the river of Your Spirit and
    my name brings honor to the Lamb.
Lord, I surrender to Your work in me; I rest my life
    within Your loving hands. . . .

Turn my heart, O Lord, like rivers of water; turn my
   heart, O Lord, by Your hand,
Till my whole life flows in the river of Your Spirit and
   my name brings honor to the Lamb.*

Little did I realize what God would have to do in my life
to begin to answer that prayer. If I had, I would most likely
never had prayed such a prayer! But during those few days, I
made that song the all-consuming cry of my heart . . . and
God began to answer that cry. But certainly not in the manner I had imagined. During the weeks that followed those
three days in the mountains, He began to *discipline* me like
He had never done before! He began to show me areas of my
heart I had never wanted to look at—things such as pride
and self-centeredness and failing to love my brother as myself.

The more He began to reveal to me, the more I felt like
a complete and absolute failure. I felt as though I'd utterly
failed my wife, my children, my congregation, and most of
all my God. As the sense of failure began to overwhelm me,
the internal pain became almost too much to bear. In the
middle of my darkest night ever, I almost lost the battle with
despair. My soul's pain was so great that I wanted to die. At
first my thoughts turned towards the shotgun in my closet,
but then towards the Bible on my nightstand. In holy des-
peration I grabbed the Bible and threw it open. It *just so
happened* that it opened to Psalm 69. In the anguish of my
spirit I began to read the prayer of another hurting, desperate soul:

Save me, O God, for the waters have come up to
my neck. I sink in the miry depths, where there is no
foothold. I have come into the deep waters; the floods

---

* DeShazo, Lynn, "Turn My Heart," Integrity's Hosanna! Music, Mobile,
Alabama, 1992.

engulf me. I am worn out calling for help; my throat is parched. My eyes fail, looking for my God. . . . You know my folly, O God; my guilt is not hidden from You.

As I continued to call out to God, I felt my spirit somehow identifying with Job's when he had made this declaration to God: *"I despise myself and repent in dust and ashes"* (42:6).

After falling back asleep in the early morning hours, I awoke a short time later only to realize that I had to go to the church office, where I was to be ready to help others find strength and comfort. As I entered my study that morning it was the last place I wanted to be. But on my desk that morning God had a gift waiting for me in my mail folder. It was a periodical that the church had been receiving for quite some time, possibly even years, although I had never subscribed to it and very seldom if ever read it. Usually it would find its way into my trash, like so many other unsolicited items. But this morning God knew I needed its message of comfort and hope.

As I opened it up, my eyes fastened upon the title of the lead article: "PAIN . . . THE GIFT THAT NOBODY WANTS." And as I gave my undivided attention to its message, I knew God Himself was giving me, His son, the encouragement that I so desperately needed. And when I had finished reading, I prayed a simple prayer: "Father, I'm not asking You to take away my pain prematurely. I want it to accomplish the work in me that You desire. But I also ask that when it has completed its appointed task that You bring me into a broad and spacious place where I may once again experience the joys of Your love." Even though the writer of Hebrews admonishes us *"not to lose heart when the Lord rebukes us,"* I had nearly given up and given in. But through the loving-kindness and grace of our heavenly Father, I found strength and hope to go on.

I recall that the Christmas holidays were just around the corner but I had no desire to join in the festal mood of the season. Now this was totally unlike me for, thanks to my parents, I had some great childhood memories of Christmas and consequently would start playing Christmas carols as early as September! I normally *loved* the holidays. But I remember that year going to the pulpit the Sunday before Christmas and, in the middle of the morning's message, I began to break down and weep. I told the congregation that this was the worst Christmas I had ever experienced. Yet I went on to say by faith that one day I would look back on this Christmas and declare it to be the best ever. I went on to explain to them how God was dealing with some issues in my life and it was very painful. I then briefly shared with them how pain truly is the gift that nobody wants, yet it is as necessary to our Christian faith as are the greatest joys.

I also came to realize that when our heavenly Father is disciplining us, Satan is right there to add to our pain. As the Father's chastening falls upon our soul, the Enemy is there to pour his salt into our wounds. The salt that he uses is condemnation. The Spirit brings *conviction*, the devil *condemnation*. Conviction is the Holy Spirit's tool to get us to confess those things that hinder our growth and injure our relationship with God. Condemnation, however, is Satan's device to keep us from turning to our heavenly Father so we might be forgiven and healed. Condemnation says, "God is through with you. He won't forgive you this time. He's tired of your shortcomings; you're nothing but a hypocrite. There's no hope for you." The voice of conviction, on the other hand, says, "I know you've failed, but I still love you and will never give up on you. Confess your sin and run to Me. I will forgive you and pick you up. I'll give you the strength to go on and the power to change. Together, we can make it!"

During this discipline/purification process, I would begin each day with this simple declaration: "Heavenly Father, You are good and You are good to me, for in Christ Jesus You have given me all good things." The reason for doing this was quite simple. I knew I needed to start each morning by declaring the goodness of God, for Satan was certainly going to be there to proclaim just the opposite! In making this declaration I was following the pattern laid out in Lamentations chapter 3: "He [God] pierced my heart with arrows from His quiver . . . my soul is downcast within me. Yet this I call to mind and therefore I have hope: Because of the Lord's great love we are not consumed, for His compassions never fail. They are new every morning; great is Your faithfulness. I say to myself, 'The Lord is my portion; therefore I will wait for Him'" (13, 20–24).

As I look back on this chapter of my life, I can now truly thank my heavenly Father that He loves me enough to discipline me. Even as the psalmist declares: "Before I was afflicted I went astray, but now I obey Your word. You are good, and what You do is good. . . . It was good for me to be afflicted" (Psalm 119:67–68, 71). Therefore, though it might again bring personal pain, my prayer to this day is still the same: *"Turn my heart, O Lord, like rivers of water; turn my heart, O Lord, by Your hand / Till my whole life flows in the river of Your Spirit and my name brings honor to the Lamb!"*

10

Moriah . . . The Manifestation of God

*A*braham was specifically commanded to take Isaac to the region of Moriah and there offer him to the Lord. There's much significance in God commanding Abraham to sacrifice Isaac there, for Moriah means *the manifestation of God* or *where God reveals Himself*. Through Abraham's prophetic act at Moriah, God's character was truly made manifest. In the Old Testament Scriptures Moriah served as the place where God most clearly revealed His nature of love. But though this story allows us a glimpse into the heart of our heavenly Father, we must realize it's only that—just a glimpse. It lacks entirely a further dimension that exists in the story of the Cross—one which causes the Abrahamic sacrifice to pale in comparison.

The element that is totally lacking in Abraham and Isaac's prophetic enactment has to do with the recipient of the sacrifice. Whereas Abraham would surrender his son to One who had proven Himself to be both loving and trustworthy, God, on the other hand, would offer up His Son for those who had consistently shown themselves to be unfaithful and unworthy. Of this truth the Apostle John writes:

"This is love: not that we loved God, but that He loved us and sent His Son as an atoning sacrifice for our sins" (1 John 4:10).

In Romans, God's sacrifice is once again placed in sharp relief with Abraham's when Paul writes, "Christ died for the ungodly. Very rarely will anyone die for a righteous man, though for a good man someone might possibly dare to die. But God demonstrates His own love for us in this: While we were still sinners, Christ died for us" (Romans 5:6–8). We might state this truth in yet another way. . . . Even though the reason for the broken relationship with our Creator lay squarely upon our shoulders, it was not man who sought restoration with God; it was God who moved towards man. Scripture is very clear on this point: "There is no one who understands, no one who seeks God. All have turned away, they have together become worthless; there is no one who does good, not even one" (Romans 3:11–12).

As we reflect upon the love and forgiveness of our heavenly Father that compelled Him to reach out to even those who were His enemies, it would be profitable to consider what our response must then be towards those who are estranged from *us*. If we would show ourselves to be true sons and daughters of God, then it would behoove us to act like Him in this matter of forgiveness. Unlike our heavenly Father, though, we often find ourselves totally unwilling to seek reconciliation with those who have injured us. We are all for the fact that God was faithful to lovingly search us out when we had turned from Him, but when it comes time for us to reach out to *our* offenders, that's an entirely different matter.

When we refuse to seek out those who have wronged us, could it be that we have forgotten these words which were written to the church at Colosse? "Bear with each other and

forgive whatever grievances you may have against one another. *Forgive as the Lord forgave you*" (Colossians 3:13). To
obey this command we must do our part in seeking healing
and restoration with our offenders. Anything short of this is
simply not *forgiving as the Lord forgave us.*

It not only depended entirely upon God to provide the
sacrifice which would allow for our reconciliation with Him,
but any hope for that reconciliation had to come at His
initiative, not ours. Remember, Scripture does not state that
we were knocking on heaven's door but rather that heaven is
knocking on ours. Jesus says, "Here I am! I stand at the door
and knock. If anyone hears My voice and opens the door, I
will come in" (Revelation 3:20).

It's comforting to know that God initiated the reconciliation process . . . and that He did so despite our sinfulness.
He loved us and sought us out when we were at our worst.
He loved us while we were quite unlovable. As much as we
would like to think otherwise, God did not set His love upon
us because He found something irresistible about us. Rather,
despite our undesirable qualities, He gave His love to us
without measure and without condition.

If we should take this thought one step further we might
appreciate even more the depths of such love. In Ephesians
5:25–26 Paul reminds every husband of Christ's great love
for His Church. Then he instructs each of them to display
this same sacrificial love to their own wives. He concludes
this thought by making it clear that it was through His unconditional love that Christ changed the very character of
His bride. So we find that when Christ chose His bride, He
actually did the unthinkable. Instead of selecting the best
heaven could offer, He chose the fallen sons of Adam. The
bride of God's Holy Son would not come from the ranks of
heaven's finest but from the pits of earth's fallen! And it

would be His unconditional love, not our unblemished character, that would one day make us His spotless bride!

How unlike the way of man. Our love states, "*I love you because you are . . .*" or "*I'll love you if you will. . . .*" Not so with God. His love is not contingent on performance or perfection. It's an unconditional love which is rooted in His unchanging nature. And it's His love that has the power to change our hearts!

In verses 31–32 of the above-mentioned passage, Paul concludes this teaching on marriage by saying something most remarkable: "'For this reason a man will leave his father and mother and be united to his wife, and the two will become one flesh.' This is a profound mystery—*but I am talking about Christ and the Church.*" Imagine that!—Christ and His followers becoming one! Just as a husband is incomplete without his wife, Christ is now incomplete without His bride. This fact alone is reason enough for us to know beyond any doubt that He is coming back for us. He who was—and forever shall be—the Son of God became the Son of Man to gain a bride for Himself. This is seen in John the Baptist's response that he gave to those who were questioning him as to why he was losing so many of his followers to Jesus. John replies: "The bride belongs to the bridegroom. The friend who attends the bridegroom waits and listens for him, and is full of joy when he hears the bridegroom's voice. That joy is mine, and it is now complete" (John 3:29). John's mission was to simply introduce the bride to the bridegroom. Once that had been accomplished, his work was done.

As our bridegroom, Christ is now incomplete without His bride, the Church. Yet it's almost inconceivable to think that God's Son should somehow be less than whole without His Church. But we must remember that this was His own doing, the decision of His own heart. Now Jesus' one great desire is to return for His bride. He longs for the day when He shall gather us unto Himself. And on that day when the King of Glory is wedded to His bride, all heaven shall rejoice! John was shown this glorious future event which he recorded for us in Revelation 19:6: "Hallelujah! For our Lord God Almighty reigns. Let us rejoice and be glad and give Him glory! For the wedding of the Lamb has come, and His bride has made herself ready. Fine linen, bright and clean, was given her to wear." This is why John writes in his first epistle to the Church, "Everyone who has this hope in him purifies himself, just as He [Christ, our bridegroom] is pure" (3:3). And why Paul writes to the church at Corinth: "I am jealous for you with a godly jealousy. I promised you to one husband, to Christ, so that I might present you as a pure virgin to Him" (2 Corinthians 11:2).

In light of this amazing love it's easy to understand why Scripture says, "How shall we escape [God's judgment] if we ignore such a great salvation?" (Hebrews 2:3). For even the immeasurable love of God cannot stop the course of justice should we choose to turn our backs on His holy sacrifice by refusing to bend our knee at the foot of the cross. Indeed, it's quite possible that even the demons of hell shall arise on Judgment Day and condemn us before God should we claim that we were unable to serve Him because we were uncertain of His love . . . we were unsure that God's Word was given with our best interests at heart . . . we were afraid that our obedience to His commands might lead to our hurt or loss.

The demons of hell could rightfully argue that, in light of the Cross, these are merely empty excuses for deliberate disobedience. They were *there* the day God sacrificed His Son. They, along with Jew and Gentile, were eyewitnesses to that hallowed scene which forever settled the question of God's love. They will surely condemn all who heard this sacred love-story yet continued with their feeble excuses as to why they could not trust God's heart and therefore would not obey His Word.

A scriptural parallel to this line of reasoning comes from the very teachings of Christ Himself. In addressing those who rejected His words, Jesus said, "The Queen of the South will rise at the judgment with the men of this generation and condemn them; for she came from the ends of the earth to listen to Solomon's wisdom, and now one greater than Solomon is here. The men of Nineveh will stand up at the judgment with this generation and condemn it; for they repented at the preaching of Jonah, and now one greater than Jonah is here" (Luke 11:31–32).

If these will be judged for rejecting the teachings of Christ, how much *more* deserving of judgment will be those who have not only rejected His words but have also spurned His *love*—a love that compelled Him to surrender His life for His foes! As we consider Moriah, the place where God manifested Himself, can we possibly have any response to His unconditional *love* other than our unconditional *surrender*?

11

"I Will Surely Bless You . . . Because You Have Obeyed Me"

*A*re there times in our own lives when we find a desire deep within to hear the voice of God calling us by name? Do we have a heartfelt longing to receive a personal directive from Him? How often have we thought, "How exciting it would be if God should choose to speak to me in a clear, audible voice"?

But as we reflect upon this story of Abraham and Isaac, we find that the word of the Lord to His servants is not always what one might consider "a word of blessing and good cheer." The day Abraham heard the Lord call his name, his heart must have leaped for joy knowing God was mindful of His humble servant. Perhaps he was expecting an added blessing for his years of faithful service. Perhaps he was waiting to hear, "Well done, good and faithful servant."

But on that momentous morning, the voice of the Lord brought Abraham a most difficult word both to understand and to obey. Quite likely his heart sank as he listened to this solemn directive from the Lord, hoping all along for a fuller explanation as to why God would require such a thing. But to his dismay he found there would be no further explanation. Yet this obedient servant of God would set his course by his Master's word. He would not vary one degree to the right or to the left until he had fully obeyed.

As Abraham raised the knife above his son, the word of the Lord came to him again. This time, though, it would bring the understanding that was absent *before* his obedience had been proven: "Now I know that you fear God, because you have not withheld from Me your son, your only son." Then for a third and final time the word of the Lord came to His faithful friend. But now it came not to bring further directives or greater understanding but rather as an oath of everlasting blessing: "I swear by Myself . . . that because you have done this . . . I will surely bless you and make your descendants as numerous as the stars in the sky and as the sand on the seashore. Your decendants will take possession of the cities of their enemies, and through your offspring all nations on earth will be blessed, *because you have obeyed Me*."

The pattern for God's dealings in Abraham's life will most likely be the same for our own: God will often issue His commands without any explanation, then await our unconditional obedience. When He's assured of this, He then grants understanding; after which He bestows upon us the promise of rich reward. But how many of us have been robbed of God's oath of blessing upon our lives, our homes and our ministries, because we failed to trust and obey? We wanted to obey, but fear, ignorance and unbelief kept us from trusting our Master's heart.

When Scripture states, "Without faith it is impossible to please God" (Hebrews 11:6), it must mean that somehow our faith brings pleasure to God. When we exercise faith like that of Abraham's—a faith which causes us to obey the voice

of our God even when it requires great personal sacrifice—
then God is able to pour out upon our lives the blessings He
so earnestly desires to give. We know that as loving and
giving parents, husbands, wives and friends, the one who
gives always derives a deeper and more satisfying joy than
the one who receives. So it is with God. "Without faith it is
impossible to please God," for without faith God is unable to
give us the gifts that cause His heart to rejoice.

But what God requires of one He does not necessarily
require of another. His dealings with His children are tai-
lored to their individual needs, fears, callings and maturity.
We must not make the mistake of basing our decisions to
obey or not to obey on what God might or might not be
asking of another. Abraham could not say, "God, You've not
required this of any other man." Though it was true that
God had not asked this of anyone else, Abraham could not
take this fact into account. When he was called to make his
decision, Abraham had to base it solely upon God's personal
dealings with him and not on the basis of God's demands on
anyone else. And so it is with all God's servants.

The Apostle Peter had to learn this biblical principle
when Jesus told him that the cost of his discipleship would
ultimately lead to his martyrdom. He then said to Peter,
"Follow Me." At this point Peter thought it might be good if
someone else was required to walk that same path—specifically his fellow disciple, John. After all, that ancient adage
"*Misery loves company*" was around in Peter's day, at least in
principle if not in word.

In response to Peter's inquiry as to the cost that John
must pay for his discipleship, Jesus said, "If I want him to
remain alive until I return, what is that to you? *You must
follow Me*" (John 21:22). At that moment Peter realized it
was the Lord alone who would determine which path each

of His disciples should take. Peter must answer the Lord's call upon his own life, not upon John's or any of the other disciples.

We know that Peter did indeed obey that call, for history records his martyrdom. As one who saw firsthand the sufferings of Christ, he knew he could never deny the reality of God's love—a love far too pure to ever be thoughtless, cruel or unjust. Thus, after witnessing his Lord and Savior surrender His life for him, he too became willing to "take up his cross and follow Christ."

Peter also learned one other invaluable lesson about the nature of that love: *The demands of God's love will always be accompanied by the riches of God's grace.* He knew that whatever God required of him, He would also grant him the strength to complete. This lesson began the very first day he met Jesus. On that occasion we find Christ declaring to Peter, "You are Simon son of John. You will be called Peter" (John 1:42). Yes, immediately after being introduced to Simon, Jesus tells him that he will be known by the name *Peter*.

However, it is important to observe that after this initial meeting, only one other time does Jesus ever again address Peter by this new name; instead, He continues to call him Simon throughout his entire time of ministry. Now that might have bothered Peter somewhat. After all, didn't Jesus Himself give him this name? Why then didn't He use it when addressing him?

It did seem to be a name of honor, for *Peter* means *rock* —someone who would be firm in character and resolve; someone you could depend on when the going got tough; someone who would neither yield to pressure nor cower to threats. It's a good possibility that Peter figured that as soon as he lived up to this new name, Jesus would begin using it.

So, in his own strength Simon struggled ever so valiantly—yet vainly—to become *Peter*. Even on the night of Christ's betrayal he was still trying to measure up to that name, for he had confidently declared that no matter what happened he would remain at Jesus' side . . . firm as a rock, standing shoulder to shoulder with Him until the bitter end. But on that fateful night when he was given not one but three chances to show his mettle, Simon proved himself to be anything but a rock. Indeed, he was as undependable as shifting sand.

We read that when Jesus needed the friendship of Peter the most, Peter let his best friend down. Luke's Gospel records that after his third denial of even knowing Christ, Jesus, being nearby, "turned and looked straight at Peter" (22:61). Immediately after the Savior's all-knowing eyes fastened upon his, Luke records that "Peter went outside and wept bitterly" (22:62). As he cried alone in the early morning hours, unable to forget the look of sorrow in his Master's eyes, he must have felt that his dreams of ever becoming *Peter, a rock,* had been lost forever through the cowardice of his own heart.

Maybe Christ had erred by saying Simon would be called Peter. Perhaps He had misread his character and had simply mistaken impetuosity for courage. Hardly . . . for upon closer examination of what Christ actually said to Simon, we find that He used the future tense and not the present when He spoke of this coming change. What Christ said was "You *will* be called Peter," not "You *now* are Peter." Simon, though, like many of us, seemed to think he must quickly live up to the challenge of this new name by relying on the strength and merits of his own feeble character. But what he had failed to realize was that only *through Christ* could he take on the nature of *Peter*—only *in Christ* could he become *a rock*.

And so early on that resurrection morning when all

seemed hopeless, the angel at the tomb spoke these words to three grieving women, "Jesus has risen! . . . Go, tell His disciples *and Peter*, 'He is going ahead of you into Galilee. There you will see Him, just as He told you'" (Mark 16:6–7). Imagine how Simon must have felt when these words were first relayed to him. Imagine his inexpressible joy upon finding that Jesus still cared about him even though knowing all he had done. Yet beyond even this, Christ's message had singled *him* out from all the other disciples . . . and in that message, He had actually called him *Peter*!

Now this was no mere slip of the angel's tongue; neither is it a scribal error. These words were carefully chosen by the Lord Himself, for through them He was relaying a message of hope to a dejected and defeated Simon by reminding him of His promise: "You will be called Peter." Think of the lift this must have given to his fallen spirit, for it meant that Jesus had not given up on one whom Satan had "sifted as wheat" nor on one who had failed his best friend.

Thus, this message was intended to not only embrace him in loving forgiveness but to also remind him of the hope to which he had been called. Now the resurrected Christ could begin His work of grace and restoration within Simon. Having been raised from the dead, He had become a "life-giving Spirit" (1 Corinthians 15:45). And in this role, Christ could now build in Simon the character of *Peter*, for this broken disciple had now come to the place where he was ready to wholly submit to the Master's touch. Through his failings he was made to clearly see the weakness and wretchedness of his own fallen nature. Peter had finally arrived at the place where he could now truly appreciate these words of Christ's: "Apart from Me you can do nothing" (John 15:5).

God gave this same promise of His unfailing love and friendship to all His children when He declared, "Never will

I leave you; never will I forsake you" (Hebrews 13:5). And just as with Peter, Christ never intended that we—through our own imperfect strength and wisdom—strive to live up to His call on our lives. "But to those whom God has called, both Jews and Greeks, Christ the power of God and the wisdom of God. . . . Therefore, as it is written: 'Let him who boasts, boast in the Lord'" (1 Corinthians 1:24, 31).

The walk of obedience for Abraham, Peter or ourselves takes us all down different paths. What God requires of one He may not necessarily demand of another. Yet if we each would trust His heart and obey His commands, regardless of the cost or consequences involved, God will surely reward our faithful obedience. And in the end, we will joyfully declare that the price of our obedience seems so small when compared with the rewards He gives both now *and in eternity*! We must always keep in mind that the fullness of our recompense will not be realized until the day of Christ's return.

Paul writes in his first letter to the church at Corinth, "If only for this life we have hope in Christ, we are to be pitied more than all men" (15:19). Paul could say this since he had spent so much of his Christian life suffering persecution from unbelieving Jews and Gentiles alike. For this very reason, he candidly admitted that if there was no hope of future reward, then all he had suffered for the sake of the gospel was in vain. His life's motto is best summed up by these words which he penned to the Philippian church: "To me, to live is Christ *and to die is gain*" (Philippians 1:21).

Now when he speaks of death being to his advantage, he is not only referring to the fact that death will end his earthly sufferings, but that the reward which awaits him shall far exceed anything he has had to undergo for the gospel's sake. To the church at Rome he writes: "I consider that our present sufferings are not worth comparing with the glory that will be revealed in us" (Romans 8:18).

Jesus Himself reaffirms this truth of future reward to the church at Smyrna: "Do not be afraid of what you are about to suffer. I tell you, the devil will put some of you in prison to test you, and you will suffer persecution for ten days. Be faithful, even to the point of death, and I will give you the crown of life" (Revelation 2:10). Therefore, there is absolutely nothing that must stand in the way of obedience to our Savior. Any price we must pay shall be more than compensated by His generous recompense.

If we should lose sight of the promises of eternity, allowing our hope to be swallowed up by the temporal, we shall place ourselves in danger of both losing our faith and becoming embittered towards God. Asaph, prophet and worship leader in ancient Israel, found himself in such a dilemna. In the Seventy-third Psalm we hear him uttering these accusatory words against his Creator—words of doubt and confusion arising from a troubled and tormented soul who had lost sight of the blessings and justice that eternity would ultimately bring:

> I envied the arrogant when I saw the prosperity of the wicked. They have no struggles; their bodies are healthy and strong. They are free from the burdens common to man; they are not plagued by human ills. Therefore pride is their necklace; they clothe themselves with violence. From their callous hearts comes iniquity; the evil conceits of their minds know no limits. . . . They say, "How can God know? Does the Most High have knowledge?" This is what the wicked are like—always carefree, they increase in wealth. Surely in vain have I kept my heart pure; in vain have I washed my hands in innocence. All day long I have been plagued; I have been punished every morning (verses 3–7, 11–14).

Asaph could no longer worship a God whom he thought was either unconcerned or unjust—a God who let the wicked prosper while allowing the righteous to suffer. But just when he was about to give way to despair, the Lord opened the eyes of his soul so he might see things as they truly were. It was then that he realized God's love would never fail him and in the end justice would prevail.

In this moment of divine revelation Asaph's worshipful spirit returns and he confidently declares:

> I am always with You; You hold me by my right hand. You guide me with Your counsel, *and afterward You will take me into glory*. Whom have I in heaven but You? And earth has nothing I desire besides You. My flesh and my heart may fail, but God is the strength of my heart *and my portion forever*. Those who are far from You will perish; You destroy all who are unfaithful to You. *But as for me, it is good to be near God* (verses 23–28).

Asaph finally realized that in spite of what appeared to be unconcern or injustice on God's part, the Lord would never allow the wicked to go unpunished nor the righteous to be removed from His presence. Only then was he able to commit himself to his faithful Creator and continue to do good. This ancient lesson which the Lord taught Asaph has been written down and faithfully preserved through the centuries for our comfort and encouragement.

Let us then look beyond the suffering of the moment which "is not worth comparing with the glory that will be revealed in us" (Romans 8:18). Let us not forget God's promise to Abraham and to those of like faith: "*I will surely bless you . . . because you have obeyed Me*" (Genesis 22:17–18).

It was several years ago while I was on a special tour of the White House that God gave me a sudden and unexpected revelation of what is to come—His kingdom that will never end. On the day of our tour, though, the President was not in. You can then understand our disappointment when our guide told our small group that if he had been in that day, we would have had the privilege of meeting him. But since he wasn't, we were instructed that we could glance through his office door, but couldn't go in. Since our guide, who was a member of the White House press corps, was a few steps ahead, I couldn't resist putting my foot just inside the door as I passed by. After all, I would then be able to say that at least I've had one foot inside the Oval Office! As we continued on the tour I became increasingly awestruck as I thought about the history and significance of this "Home of the Presidents." However, I knew I would never really be a part of its story. I knew I would always remain just another person who had toured this historic seat of political power. I found that these thoughts produced in me both a hint of envy and also a feeling of insignificance. But right at that very instant I sensed these words being spoken to my heart: "You may never be a part of the power base of this nation. But don't let that trouble you. Soon the United States of America will go the way of all previous nations and empires. This government is soon to end. This nation's days are numbered. But if you will be faithful to Me, I'll make you a part of My kingdom that shall *never* end—I promise that you will reign with Me for all eternity!" Needless to say, my whole perspective on what was really important in this life changed in an instant! I trust that I will never forget that moment.

Now lest you think that this word has no meaning for you, listen closely to what the King of kings declares to everyone of His servants in Revelation 2:26–27: "To him who overcomes and does My will to the end, I will give authority over the nations—'He will rule them with an iron scepter; He will dash them to pieces like pottery'—just as I have received authority from My Father."

In this life you and I may never be elected to any important political office or ever be appointed to any high governmental position . . . but on the authority of God's Word let me assure you, that as obedient sons and daughters of the Most High, we shall all one day be a part of His kingdom that will never pass away!

12

He Was Called God's Friend

No higher honor could be given anyone than the tribute paid Abraham: "He was called God's friend" (James 2:23). But how does one become a friend of God? Though quite often the promise of money, power or fame can buy the friendship of man, we must not be led to conclude that friendship with man's Creator is also for sale. It would be utterly foolish for any to believe that God's friendship could ever be purchased at any price. Besides, what truly effective enticement could a creature of dust offer the King of the universe?

Yet as foolish as it is to think we might buy the friendship of God, it's just as harmful to hold the false assumption that intimacy with our Creator is both unattainable and unthinkable. From the very beginning God Himself made it clear that He wanted more than simply a Creator/creature relationship with man. We immediately find evidence of this when noting how our Creator chose to fashion us. God would not have made us in His image if it were not for the fact that He desired man to be more than just another among His many creatures. And when He granted us the freedom of choice, He placed into our relationship one of the essential building blocks of every true friendship. Without the right of individual choice, friendship can never be anything more than a meaningless concept.

As we read past the creation account, we learn that sometime in the late afternoon on the very day of man's fall, God came down to walk in Eden's garden. Because of this small but significant observation which the Holy Spirit obviously considered important enough to include, we can safely assume that this was not an unusual thing for God to do. For not only do we find Him appearing there on the very day of the Fall but, even without their having seen Him, Adam and Eve knew it was the Lord. Therefore, it would be proper to conclude that the latter part of the day was God's set time to come and talk with His friends. These visits on God's part are one more indication that our Creator did in fact desire to fellowship with those whom He had made in His likeness. He wanted to be our friend as well as our Creator. So we mustn't think that friendship with God is out of the question, for quite the contrary is true.

Throughout this book, we've focused primarily upon God's love for man. And as seen clearly in Scripture, this love is unconditional. From the opening pages of the Bible we find that it is this unconditional love which compels our Creator to untiringly seek out the fallen sons of Adam. Even though all of us had gone our own way, it was this love that caused Him to sacrifice everything for our redemption.

Neither is God's unconditional love just a theological concept void of any individual or personal application. For once again, early in earth's history we find God reaching out to not only the fallen *sons* of Adam but specifically to *a* fallen *son* of Adam, *Cain*—teaching us that our Creator is truly concerned about each individual. However, with just a superficial reading of the story of Cain and Abel, the unconditional love which God extends to Cain can easily pass unnoticed.

The Scriptures tell us, "The Lord looked with favor on Abel and his offering, but on Cain and his offering He did not" (Genesis 4:4–5). The reason for the different reception of the two offerings appears to lie not in the fact that Abel brought a blood sacrifice and Cain a bloodless one, for each brought a gift from his own labor; rather, Abel pleased God because he offered the first and the *best* of his flock (Genesis 4:4), whereas Cain failed to honor his Maker and Provider because he did not bring the first fruits and the best of his crops but only "*some* of the fruits of the soil" (v. 3).

Again, with just a cursory reading of this account we might overlook the fact that though God was not pleased with either Cain's actions or his offering, He did not turn His back on him. In fact, quite the contrary is true, for it tells us that God sought out a rebellious and angry Cain. And when He confronted him, it was with loving concern. Listen to how the Creator tries to reach the heart of this fallen son: "Why are you angry? Why is your face downcast? If you do what is right, will you not be accepted?" (Genesis 4:6–7). By extending to Cain the hope of divine acceptance, God wanted him to know that though his *offering* was rejected, *he* was not. Otherwise, God would not have urged him to deal with what was destroying their relationship. He would have simply written him off. So after a careful reading of this account, we can see in both God's actions and words the loving heart of a caring Father striving to touch a rebellious son.

Let's consider one other example that powerfully illustrates this unconditional love of our heavenly Father—a love that values and cares for each individual.

While surrounded by the luxuries of the palace and the

splendor of his domain, King David falls to the temptation of adultery and then attempts to hide it by having the unsuspecting husband slaughtered on the field of battle. For quite some time, David believes he has been successful in his cover-up. But God loves David too much for his sin to remain hidden. His unconditional love will not let David go. God's heart is broken—not just from the pain that David's sin has brought to others but also by the unconfessed sin that has now severed their fellowship. Brokenhearted, God now sends the prophet Nathan to penetrate the hardened heart of His once tender servant. Nathan's mission is successful. *David's heart is finally broken and his sin is confessed.*

Here we are taught that even though David refused to acknowledge his sin, God's great love would not allow Him to wait idly by for David to perhaps come to his senses. Though David seemed able to ignore their severed relationship, God could not; the pain of separation was too great for a loving God. The wedge of sin driven between them was like a giant stake pounded into the Father's heart. The daily communion that God so enjoyed with His shepherd-king had ended. David no longer could bring his songs of worship and praise before the Creator's throne. The harp that once was alive with the music of love now lay covered in dust. For this reason, God's unconditional love compelled Him to do all in His power to restore their broken friendship.

These stories of Cain and David are just two of many which undeniably prove the unconditional love of our Creator for every individual. *But although God's love is unconditional, His friendship is not.* Jesus Himself teaches this truth most clearly in the 15th chapter of John's Gospel. Among the many things He shares in this passage, perhaps the statement He makes in the 13th verse is the one most quoted: "Greater love has no one than this, that he lay down his life for his friends" (John 15:13). But what is not often quoted is the verse that immediately follows. Yet without it, we have only half of what Christ was saying. What comes after actually completes the thought: "You are My friends, if you do what I command" (John 15:14).

From this teaching of Christ's, we clearly see that there is a condition to becoming God's friend. It's called *obedience*. That's why it's so important for us to lay the foundation of God's *unconditional love*, for it is only upon this foundation that we can unhesitatingly place our *unconditional obedience*. And it's only our unconditional obedience that qualifies us, as with Abraham of old, to be called God's friend.

To further illustrate the necessity of obedience for the privilege of divine friendship, we need only to look at the preceding verses of John 15: "As the Father has loved Me, so have I loved you. Now remain in My love. If you obey My commands, you will remain in My love, just as I have obeyed My Father's commands and remain in His love" (John 15:9–10). Here Jesus equates friendship with the concept of remaining in His love . . . and remaining in His love, with obedience. This is not to say that if we're disobedient God no longer loves us, for we've already established the fact that His love is unconditional. But it does mean that we've walked away from fellowship with Him. No longer can we say that our *friendship* with God is intact. As John says in his first epistle, "If we claim to have fellowship with Him yet walk in the darkness [i.e., disobedience], we lie and do not live by the truth. But if we walk in the light, as He is in the light, we have fellowship with one another . . ." (1 John 1:6–7).

At Jesus' baptism, the Father declared, "This is My Son, whom I love; with Him I am well pleased" (Matthew 3:17). The key to what the Father is saying here is found in those last two words, "*well pleased*." That's what it means to "*re-*

138 · Trusting God's Heart When You Can't Trace His Hand

main in God's love"; that's what it means to be called "*God's friend*." There's a vast amount of difference between God loving us unconditionally and God being "well pleased" with us. One has to do with His nature alone, the other with the pleasure that we bring Him by our loving obedience.

One of the greatest gifts children can give their parents is the joy they bring them when they're obedient. As John the beloved writes, "I have no greater joy than to hear that my children are walking in the truth" (3 John 4). Here John is expressing the Father-heart of God. Our heavenly Father is well pleased with us when, as His children, we respond in unconditional obedience to His unconditional love.

Though God will always love us, it does not mean that He will always delight in us. A prime example of this is found in the stern admonition Jesus gives to His church at Laodicea: "I know your deeds, that you are neither cold nor hot. I wish you were either one or the other! So, because you are lukewarm—neither hot nor cold—I am about to spit you out of my mouth. . . . Those whom I love I rebuke" (Revelation 3:15–16, 19). Now that's a pretty passionate way of telling them that if they don't make the necessary changes, their friendship will come to an abrupt end! Certainly Christ was not "well pleased" with the Laodicean Christians. He had no reason to "delight" in them. Again, it was His unconditional love that made Him so passionate about their friendship.

Before concluding our remarks on friendship with our Creator, I believe we would find it helpful to consider two blessings given to those who, by their obedience, have elected to be called God's friends.

First, as we look again at Christ's teachings about "remaining in His love" we find Him immediately thereafter telling us of the primary benefit which would accompany such action: "I have told you this so that My joy may be in you and that your joy may be complete" (John 15:11). Jesus wanted us to follow Him on the path of obedience so the joy that He Himself possessed might also be ours. Thus, obedience not only brings joy to our heavenly Father, but also to His obedient children.

Long ago the psalmist spoke of the joy which the Father would bestow upon His only begotten Son: "You have loved righteousness and hated wickedness; therefore God, Your God, has set You above Your companions by anointing You with the oil of joy" (Psalm 45:7 and Hebrews 1:9). This is the same joy that Jesus was referring to in John 15:11. This is the joy that He now wants *us* to experience. Here we are clearly told why God poured out His joy upon His Son: "He *loved righteousness* and *hated wickedness*." Jesus was "anointed" by His Father with the oil of *joy*, for daily He lived His life in loving submission to His Father's will.

Joy then was simply the by-product of His obedience, of remaining in His Father's love. He did not obtain joy by directly pursuing it, but it was poured out upon Him as He faithfully went about His Father's business. Jesus felt no need to seek joy. He only felt the need to do His Father's will. How unlike the world's advice that would tell us that if we are to find happiness, then we'd be wise to look out for our own interests and get whatever we can whenever we can. But God's ways are not man's ways. Proverbs 16:25 makes this abundantly clear when it states, "There is a way that seems right to a man, but in the end it leads to death."

How many of us have lost something of significant value and ended up spending many fruitless hours trying to find it? After several days and possibly weeks of mounting frustration, we finally gave up. We believed it was lost forever and sadly resigned ourselves to that fact. Rather than searching any longer, we went about the necessary business of the day. Then a most remarkable thing occurred: In the midst of our daily endeavors we happened upon the very object we had searched so long to find. Such is the joy of God's kingdom. When we cease looking for "joy" and turn to do the Father's will, then and only then shall we find the joy that seemed so illusive.

Jesus was not dependent upon anything or anyone for His joy. Therefore, nothing or no one could ever rob Him of it. As someone wisely noted, *"Any happiness that one can give, one can also take away."* But for those who, like Christ, derive their joy from an everlasting, ever-loving and ever-faithful God, their joy can never be taken away.

As we consider now the second major benefit that comes from being God's friend, once again we find that it is most clearly articulated in the 15th chapter of John. Here Jesus tells His disciples: "I no longer call you servants, because a servant does not know his master's business. Instead, I have called you friends, for everything that I learned from My Father I have made known to you" (John 15:15). In this verse Jesus lets His disciples know that He considers them more than just servants—He counts them among His friends. The main distinction that Jesus draws here between being one's servant or being one's friend resides primarily in whether or not they are privy to the plans, decisions and considerations of the other. If they are not a part of this process, then they are not considered a friend but a servant.

As we look back on the life of Abraham, "the friend of God," we can see how this was indeed the case. Before God destroyed Sodom and Gomorrah, He informed Abraham what He was intending to do. Abraham then had the opportunity to talk this over with his friend (Genesis 18). And on the basis of this friendship, God listened to Abraham. He granted him his every request over the number of righteous people needed to be found within these cities if they were to be spared. And though there was not found this minimal number, even after their destruction Scripture is careful to point out the ongoing effects of Abraham's friendship with God: "So when God destroyed the cities of the plain, *He remembered Abraham*, and He brought Lot out of the catastrophe that overthrew the cities where Lot had lived" (Genesis 19:29).

As it was with Abraham, so Christ promises it shall be with His disciples. He tells them that He has and will share with them the very thoughts and purposes of His Father. He then goes on to say, in this and the succeeding chapter, that after His return to the Father, the promised Holy Spirit will be sent in His name for the very purpose of continuing this all-important aspect of their friendship. Of the Spirit's work Jesus says: "But when He, the Spirit of truth, comes, He will guide you into all truth. He will not speak on His own; He will speak only what He hears, and He will tell you what is yet to come. He will bring glory to Me by taking from what is Mine and making it known to you. All that belongs to the Father is Mine. This is why I said the Spirit will take from what is Mine and make it known to you" (John 16:13–15).

It is of vital importance that we know this truth which the Holy Spirit would reveal to us in Jesus' name. For earlier in John's Gospel, Jesus promised that it would be this truth which would *set us free—free to become all God would have us be in Christ*. Keep in mind, though, that the Holy Spirit is not sent as a teacher of truth to mankind in general but only to those who are God's friends. It is to His disciples, His *friends*, that Jesus promises, "He [the Spirit] will guide you into all truth."

However, lest we assume that all who believe Jesus' words

are automatically His disciples and therefore His friends, let us look at the entire quote from this earlier passage that promises us freedom. Then let us carefully consider what Jesus said and to whom He said it: "To the Jews who had believed Him, Jesus said, 'If you hold to My teaching, you are really My disciples. Then you will know the truth, and the truth will set you free'" (John 8:31–32). Note that even though these Jews had believed Christ, He did not for this reason alone include them as disciples. Rather, He told them that they must now "*hold to His teaching*" if they would prove themselves to be authentic disciples. They must not simply be "hearers" of His word . . . they must also be "doers" of His word. And it was to these that He promised, "*Then* you will know the truth and the truth will set you free."

It was man's *disobedience* to the truth that first brought him into sin's bondage, and now it would be his *obedience* to the truth that would set him free . . . free to be all that God had intended him to be! Christ has promised to all His friends, to all His disciples, the liberating knowledge that only His Spirit can bring. As it is written, "Now the Lord is the Spirit, and where the Spirit of the Lord is, there is freedom" (2 Corinthians 3:17).

God is truly "no respecter of persons" (Acts 10:34), a shower of favoritism. His heart's one desire has always been that each, like Abraham, be called His friend. But He knew that without our complete trust in His loving character, obedience would be most improbable and, unlike Abraham, we could never be called God's friend. So in the Cross, God gave us every reason to trust His love and be His friend. After witnessing its horrors, none could rightfully question God's loving intentions towards man. Through the sacrifice of His Holy Lamb, God made it possible for each of us to trust His heart. The purity and depth of our Creator's love, demonstrated through His supreme sacrifice, assures us that He is a friend who will always act in our best interests. And because friendship with God means friendship with the One who is *eternal*, it, like He, shall never die. These words shall forever stand as a tribute to all who, like Abraham, trusted God's heart when they couldn't trace His hand: "*I do not call you My servants*," declares the Lord. "*I call you My friends.*"

Finally, what God requires of one friend, He may not necessarily demand of another. Yet the command that each must ultimately obey, regardless of the cost involved, is that which has always been required of everyone who would please Him: "Love the Lord your God with all your heart and with all your soul and with all your strength" (Deuteronomy 6:5). To love the Lord our God with all our heart, soul and strength means we will relinquish all that we are and all that we have to His divine directives. Any less of a commitment only shows we do not truly understand the greatest of all commands.

In her story "*The Treasure,*"* Alice Gray reaches into the depths of our emotions as she movingly conveys the response of a loving father's heart to the sacrifice of his beloved daughter:

> The cheerful girl with bouncy golden curls was almost five. Waiting with her mother at the checkout stand, she saw them—a circle of glistening white pearls in a pink foil box. "Oh please, Mommy. Can I have them? Please, Mommy, PLEASE!" Quickly the mother checked the back of the little foil box and then looked back into her little girl's upturned face. "A dollar ninety-five. That's almost two dollars. If you really want them I'll think of some extra chores for you and in no time you can save enough money to buy them for yourself. Your birthday's only a week away and you might get

---

* From *Stories for the Heart, the Second Collection*, Alice Gray, Multnomah Publishers, Sisters, Oregon.

another crisp dollar bill from Grandma." As soon as Jenny got home, she emptied her penny bank and counted seventeen pennies. After dinner, she did more than her share of chores and then went to the neighbor and asked Mrs. McJames if she could pick dandelions for ten cents.

On her birthday, Grandma did give her another new dollar bill and at last she had enough money to buy the necklace. Jenny loved her pearls. They made her feel dressed up and grown up. She wore them everywhere—Sunday school, kindergarten, even to bed. The only time she took them off was when she went swimming or had a bubble bath. Mother said if they got wet, they might turn her neck green.

Jenny had a very loving daddy and every night when she was ready for bed, he would stop whatever he was doing and come upstairs to read her a story. One night when he finished the story, he asked Jenny, "Do you love me?" "Oh yes, Daddy. You know that I love you." "Then give me your pearls," he replied. "Oh, Daddy, not my pearls. But you can have Princess—the white horse from my collection—the one with the pink tail. Remember, Daddy? The one you gave me. She's my favorite." "That's okay, Honey. Daddy loves you. Good night," and he brushed her cheek with a kiss.

About a week later, after the story time, Jenny's daddy asked again, "Do you love me?" "Daddy, you know I love you." "Then give me your pearls." "Oh, Daddy, not my pearls. But you can have my baby doll. The brand new one I got for my birthday. She's so beautiful and you can have the yellow blanket that matches her sleeper." "That's okay. Sleep well. God bless you, little one. Daddy loves you." And, as always, he brushed her cheek with a gentle kiss.

A few nights later when her daddy came in, Jenny was sitting on her bed with her legs crossed Indian-style. As he came close, he noticed her chin was trembling and one silent tear rolled down her cheek. "What is it, Jenny? What's the matter?" Jenny didn't say anything but lifted her little hand up to her daddy. And when she opened it, there was her little pearl necklace. With a quiver, she finally said, "Here, Daddy, it's for you." With tears gathering in his own eyes, Jenny's daddy reached out with one hand to take the dime-store necklace, and with the other hand he reached into his pocket and pulled out a blue velvet case with a strand of genuine pearls and gave them to Jenny. He had had them all the time. He was just waiting for her to give up the dime-store stuff so he could give her genuine treasure.

Can we trust our Father's heart? Could we doubt our Savior's love? In light of Calvary's sacrifice, and the grace that comes through Christ, our response to His every command must always and forever be: "I will obey You, O God, even when I don't understand Your ways. I will gladly surrender all you require of me, for I know You're too kind to ever be cruel and too wise to ever make a mistake. Though I might not always be able to trace Your hand, I can always trust Your heart. Compelled by Your love, You raised the knife to slay Your Son—Your only Son. And when that knife had found its mark, Your bruised and bleeding Son drew His final breath and cried, 'It is finished,' while horrified angels bowed their heads in holy silence and You closed tear-filled eyes and wept alone. I know, O God, that You love me, for You did not withhold from me Your Son—Your only Son! Now when I find myself surrounded by the darkness of uncertainty, the light of Your love will enable me to stand firm in my faith. And when the Prince of Darkness comes to question the loving intentions of Your heart, I shall boldly and confidently proclaim what even he knows to be true: 'Jesus loves me, this I know!' "

"I pray that you, being rooted and established in love, may have power, together with all the saints, to grasp how wide and long and high and deep is the love of Christ, and to know this love that surpasses knowledge—that you may be filled to the measure of all the fullness of God" (Ephesians 3:17–19).